WE DON'T MAKE OURSELVES SMALLER HERE

Megan Jayne Crabbe is a bestselling author, content creator and presenter. With over a million followers, Megan is best known for her work in body positivity: using social media to help change the narrative of how women feel about their bodies. Megan wrote her first book, *Body Positive Power*, in 2017, and has given keynotes and hosted workshops across the world. Megan is also a presenter and host, working with major broadcasters like BBC, Universal Studios, Channel 4 and MTV.

WE DON'T MAKE OURSELVES SMALLER HERE

Reclaiming All That's Rightfully Ours

MEGAN JAYNE CRABBE

First published in Great Britain in 2025 by Hodder Catalyst
An imprint of Hodder & Stoughton Limited
An Hachette UK company

The authorised representative in the EEA is Hachette Ireland, 8 Castlecourt Centre,
Dublin 15, D15 XTP3, Ireland (email: info@hbgi.ie)

1

Illustrations by Kelly Bastow

A CIP catalogue record for this title is available from the British Library

Hardback ISBN 9781399738064
Trade Paperback ISBN 9781399738071
ebook ISBN 9781399738088

Typeset in Celeste by Manipal Teechnologies Limited

Printed and bound in Great Britain by Clays Ltd, Elcograf S.p.A.

Hodder & Stoughton policy is to use papers that are natural, renewable and
recyclable products and made from wood grown in sustainable forests. The logging
and manufacturing processes are expected to conform to the environmental
regulations of the country of origin.

Hodder & Stoughton Limited
Carmelite House
50 Victoria Embankment
London EC4Y 0DZ

www.hoddercatalyst.co.uk

CONTENTS

Introduction   ix
BODY
    Thin   3
    On Eating in Public   18
    Movement   29
    The Pretty Tax   36
    What Naturally Grows   47
HEART
    When It's Time to Leave   60
    The Dating Games   85
    Being Saved   103
    Good Love   116
SEXUALITY
    Coming Out   125
    What Feels Good   135
    Sluthood   146
    The Script   162
LIFE
    The Path   172
    Children   178
    Fame   188
    The Productivity Trap   200
    Getting Life Wrong   208
SELF
    Identity   221
    Good Personhood   230
    Likeability   243
    Self-Love   260

Acknowledgements   265
Endnotes   267

*To all the women who refuse to make themselves
small in a world determined to shrink us –
thank you.*

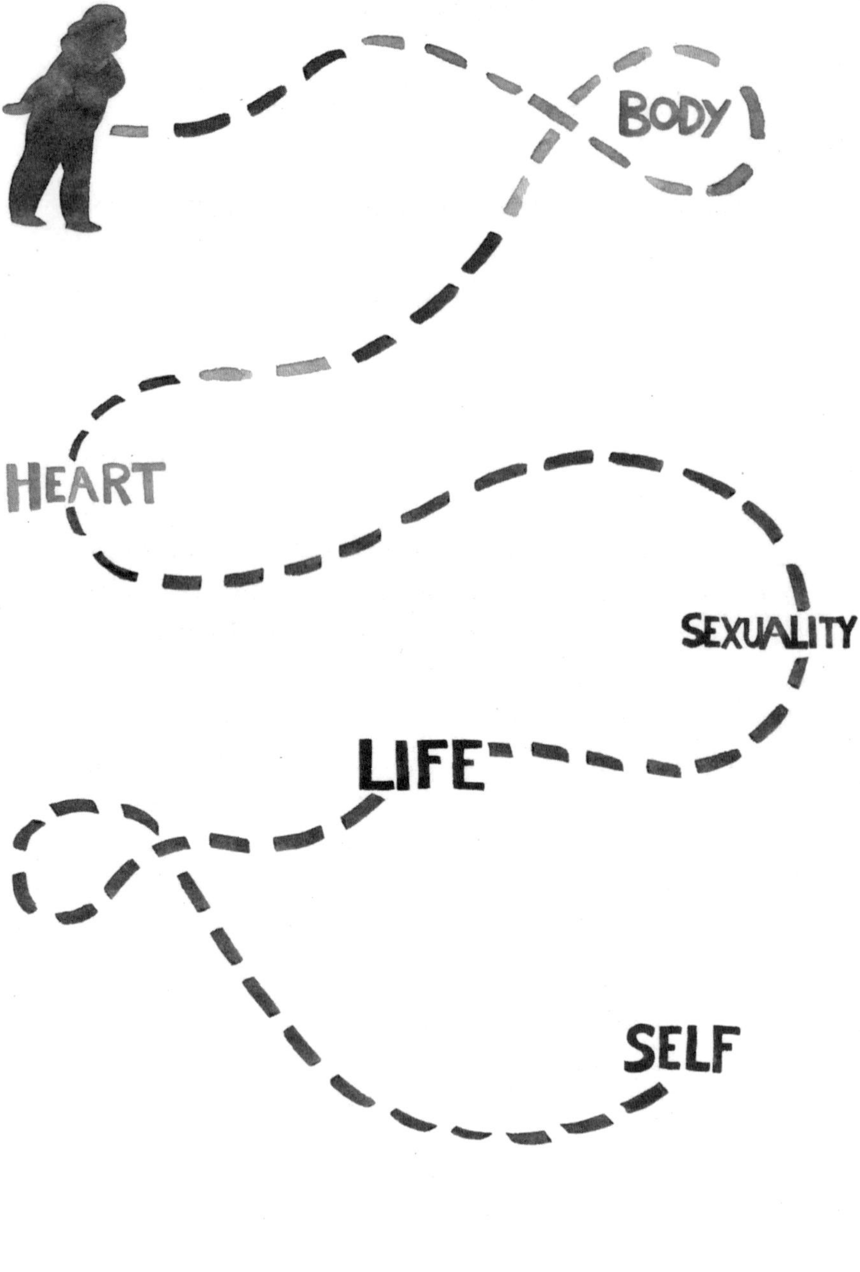
BODY
HEART
SEXUALITY
LIFE
SELF

INTRODUCTION

Imagine a world where we were never taught to make ourselves small.

In that world, we get to hold onto the wonder and appreciation for our bodies that we had when we were born. There is no diet culture, no exclusionary beauty standards to convince us that our appearance is wrong. We would spend our days moving our bodies freely and unapologetically through public space, embracing our natural form.

We would be free of the male gaze, and all the ways it weighs us down. What if we were never convinced to look for validation in places outside of ourselves? Imagine if we really knew our worth, and didn't stay in relationships or situations where it wasn't recognised. We wouldn't be waiting for romantic love to save us; we would be romancing ourselves. We could shake off the sexual shame that our patriarchal culture has burdened us with for so long. We would be free to explore safely, getting to know ourselves – deeply and intimately – in every way.

In another world, we respect that people are all different, and there would be no uniform life path. Everyone would be entitled to make their own choices without comparison or pressure, and we wouldn't reduce people's value to 'output' and how productive or wealthy they are. We would exist authentically and build unshakeable self-esteem. We wouldn't abandon ourselves when someone doesn't like us because we would like ourselves first. In fact, we would love ourselves fiercely, and treat ourselves as such.

That's the world I want for us, one where we can be our biggest selves. Although I recognise that it's a long way from where we are right now.

In *this* world, we have been making ourselves small for most of our lives: shrinking our bodies to chase impossible ideals, suppressing our needs to not burden other people, apologising too much and accepting less than we deserve. We've stayed where our value isn't appreciated, felt shame for our natural desires, forced ourselves into expectations that don't fit us, and allowed other people to define who we are.

None of this has been our fault – we've adapted to survive in our surroundings. We've been navigating systems that weren't designed with us in mind, and absorbing endless cultural messages that do more harm than we realise. *Of course,* we make ourselves small, it's the only way we believe we're allowed to be. How would we even begin to learn something different or change the way we feel?

I'm not going to pretend that I have all the answers. This isn't a step-by-step guide to help you miraculously become your boldest, most authentic self. But it is an invitation to come with me and explore some of the places where parts of us were lost, taken or given away. Maybe, we can take them back. Maybe we can give ourselves permission to be just a little bit bigger, a little less apologetic, a little more fully ourselves.

As I'm sure is the case for many of you reading this, the first part of myself that I was convinced to turn against was my body. It took twenty years of moving through various stages of shame and disorder before I would come anywhere close to reclaiming her. If you've read my first book, *Body Positive Power*, you'll know everything I had to unlearn to get here. I'm starting with the body once again because I don't think I'm alone in losing her first. I think that reclaiming the vessel we live in lays the groundwork for taking back so much more.

I've written about my personal experience of navigating womanhood within patriarchy, so a lot of the language is gendered. However, if your identity is different to mine and you still relate to what's in these pages, you are of course welcome here. Our experience is expansive and there's room for us all.

Even though I want us to feel empowered to be our biggest selves, I recognise the limitations of focusing on the self. Unfortunately (for now) we still have to exist within the same systems that made us small, and that's what truly needs to change. But I do believe there's value in starting with us. We might not change the whole world, but we can change our worlds – and every change has to start somewhere.

We deserve to reclaim everything that's rightfully ours: our bodies, our hearts, our sexuality, our lives, our whole selves. We never should have been taught to make ourselves small. It's time we come home to ourselves, and realise that we were always meant to be more.

BODY

HEART

SEXUALITY

LIFE

SELF

BODY

Once upon a time we worshipped the impossible…
Whatever ratio of waist to hip was 'in',
We spent lifetimes gazing at pinched and
stretched pages,
And closed our ~~legs~~ mouths to stay free from sin.
We frankensteined a new dream with every season:
Those legs, their arms, this nose, that arse,
Thankfully the gurus promising to stitch us together
    accepted all major credit cards.
The memories of spinning in golden fields somehow
    were stripped from our minds,
We moved only for results, in windowless grey rooms,
Before apologising for the sweat left behind.
We turned mirrors into microscopes and carved
    out flaws,
Prayed to win the morning weigh-in like a lottery
    being drawn.
We passed billboards that called us failures and went
    about our day,
Twisted and squeezed when they looked and learned
    to shrink under their gaze.
When headlines screamed "you can do it, too!",
We held now between our fingers and let it slip through.

1

WE DON'T MAKE OURSELVES SMALLER HERE

And it wasn't just our own flesh we held together
    with shame,
Everybody needs a scapegoat; another body to
    blame.
We turned our flowers into weeds where they
naturally grew,
Swallowed wants, abandoned needs – don't mean to
    bother // – didn't mean to
Overlaid every image with cartoon eyes, unreal skin,
Compared ourselves to lies and forgeries and
Made enemies out of kin
At the end of it all when we were smaller than
    small with
Canyons between ourselves and the shells we live in
We looked up to realise: it was never enough
There was never a prize of perfect beauty to win.
Shall we begin the unlearning? We trembled to ask,
Clinging tight to how we've always been...
But something like hunger, raised from our depths
Has finally awoken to every lie we've seen.
So we unstitch with rage and say yes to flavour,
We laugh when they come to sell the next cure,
The numbers are banished, the competition called off,
We refuse to keep making ourselves small.
With tender regret we tend to our wounds:
The wasted years and flesh full of thorns,
We soothe, we feed, we move, we forgive,
We come home to ourselves, reborn.
Here is our shelter. Here is our guide. Here is
    our vehicle
For the rest of our lives these bodies are ours and
We are theirs and there is no greater miracle
That could ever be asked for.

THIN

The nights would always be the same.

Homework finished, dinner dissected as Nickelodeon filled the living room, a bedtime ritual of cleaning teeth and choosing a Beanie Baby to sleep next to before climbing into well-worn floral sheets. Then it was only me, my imagination, and the place we would go each evening.

Eyes closed, night light humming in the background, I would force a vision of my future self into the space of my mind: how I would look in fifteen years' time, after I'd left adolescence behind.

She was tall, with long shining limbs that cut gracefully through the air, always poised and ready. She was stylish – the best of Barbie's wardrobe in real size, effortlessly cool. She had a dazzling smile and bright sparkling eyes – blue, usually. Her satin hair bounced breezily down her shoulders, a stray golden wave brushing a collarbone. Her hips swayed with the natural step of the heels she wore every day. Her lips were glossed. Her lashes coated. She was a picture-perfect model of what my womanhood could be.

In case it isn't clear, above everything else, in a realm of importance all its own: she was thin. Thinner than my soft and solid childhood body had ever allowed me to be.

The projection wasn't based on how I might realistically look when I grew up – the blonde hair and blue eyes of the fantasy clashed with the dark features I'd inherited from my Afro-Caribbean father. Nobody in the family was particularly tall, either. It was a vision pieced together from countless images of culturally confirmed beauty: cover girls and popstars and plastic dolls. My future self was two parts Christina Aguilera and one part Rachel Green, with a sprinkling of Britney for good measure.

I willed her to life every night, vowing that I would do whatever I had to do to become her. It was non-negotiable – I would be thin, and beautiful, and there was no other option to consider, not if I wanted the life that goes along with being thin and beautiful.

In that life, I would be popular. Friends would flock to my side, ask for my advice, invite me places, be there all the time. I would be successful – floating through any doors that held opportunity inside, naturally finding the spotlight, gliding into the glamourous life. I would be desired – showered with attention, worshipped by men, fairytale romances one after the other. And, of course, I would be happy. Happy like they all were, always smiling, always having adventures, always wanted for something or by someone.

Life happened to the thin and beautiful, and I wanted life to happen to me. The only thing getting in the way was my body, and how ugly and wrong it seemed to be. I would have to change it all: my hair, my legs, my stomach, my face. *They can do anything with plastic surgery these days*, my eight-year-old brain surmised each night, as we drifted into a wishful sleep.

In the meantime, I could start on the biggest problem myself. I knew how to do it – I'd read the diet articles that listed 'good' and 'bad' foods, I'd seen the numbers on the side of all the packets, I'd heard the conversations about the best ways to lose weight, I knew how to use the bathroom scales. I could eat less. I had the will power. I would make my body smaller. I had to.

It was non-negotiable.

* * *

When I tell people how young I was when I first started feeling like my body was wrong (five years old, primary school, I was the only chubby mixed-race girl in the class), they're usually shocked. *How could a child of that age be aware of these things?* I tell them, with a resigned shrug of my shoulders, that it's more common than you might think.

A study by the University of Castilla-La Mancha suggests that more than half of girls aged three to six years old are dissatisfied with their body and are showing signs of wanting to be thinner.[1] In the UK, Common Sense Media reported that 80% of ten-year-old girls have been on a diet.[2] We learn, as soon as we're old enough to start absorbing the messages and images of our culture, that a smaller body is a better body. The messages and images are *everywhere*.

Our fairytale heroines and favourite dolls are thin.

I remember gazing into the crystal blue of Cinderella's gown, fantasising about one day looking as elegant, as delicate as she did. Pocahontas was the closest thing I had to representation as a little girl with light brown skin, but she was so lean, so lithe, limbs scaling clifftops effortlessly, waist mesmerizingly cinched. I dreamed of having a waist so small...

When the waist-to-hip ratio of eleven popular Disney princesses was measured in a 2019 study, the researchers reached an average figure of 0.535 – meaning that the princesses' waist measurements are almost half the size of their hips and according to the authors of the study 'nearly impossible to achieve naturally'.[3] The World Health Organisation estimates a 'moderate' waist-to-hip ratio for women to be around 0.85.[4] We are idolising the impossible before we're old enough to know it.

The messages we absorb don't only teach us to see thinness as desirable, they teach us to see fatness as the worst possible physical trait.

Whilst the princesses and their unobtainable proportions are associated with goodness, virtue and happily-ever-afters, the prevalence of plus-size villains (think: Ursula in *The Little Mermaid,* the Queen of Hearts in *Alice in Wonderland),* aligns having a larger body with unhappiness, lack of morals, evil. Fatphobia starts to seep in early.

In 2016, Mattel made headlines for releasing a new, more diverse range of Barbie dolls, with three new body types including 'curvy'. It was a long overdue step in the right direction, given the measurements of the original Barbie are so unrealistic that when blown up to life-size, the doll would fit the weight criteria for an anorexia diagnosis and would have to walk on all fours, being unable to support her own proportions standing up.[5] Curvy Barbie is at least *slightly* more realistic, coming in at a UK size 6/8 (US size 2/4 or EU size 34/36). Original Barbie is a UK size 2 (US size oo or EU size 30).

When girls were presented with the full range of Barbies – original, tall, petite and curvy – and asked to assign positive or negative traits to the dolls in one 2019 study, they were much more likely to have negative attitudes towards the curvy doll – she was also the one they were least interested in playing with.[6] The title of the study reads "You can buy a child a Curvy Barbie doll, but you can't make her like it" – not when she's already internalised the thin ideal from the cultural messaging all around her.

Our leading ladies and main characters are thin.

I grew up watching the women of *Friends* shrink with each season. My tween Disney idols – Demi Lovato, Miley Cyrus, Vanessa Hudgens, Lindsay Lohan – all embodied an ideal that seemed to get smaller and smaller with each movie (many of them have since spoken out about eating disorders, body image issues and struggles with mental health throughout their careers). In the realm of reality TV, judges on *America's Next Top Model* were labelling slim models as plus size and shows like *What Not to Wear, Supersize Vs Superskinny* and *The Biggest Loser* were built on body shaming and fatphobia.

During my adolescence, the on-screen presence of the thin ideal was relentless. *Sex and the City, 90210, Gossip Girl, Buffy the Vampire Slayer, Desperate Housewives, The O.C.* and beyond all reinforced the narrative that only women below a UK size 10 (US size 6/EU size 38) were worthy of primetime storylines, and Hollywood movies weren't any better. When fat characters were present, they were most likely being played by thin actors wearing a fat suit as a comedic device: Courtney Cox as Fat Monica, Gwyneth Paltrow in *Shallow Hal*, Eddie Murphy in *The Nutty Professor*.

Sure, we were offered *Bridget Jones* and *Ugly Betty* as more relatable on-screen heroines, but neither Renée Zellweger nor America Ferrera deviated *too far* from the ideal. Bridget is a UK size 12 (US size 8/EU size 40) who is obsessed with losing weight. Betty isn't *that* much bigger than her fatphobic co-workers who ridicule her size, style and eating habits in nearly every episode. The way these women were framed as falling miles outside the beauty standard perfectly captures how brainwashed we all were by the thin ideal.

The 90s and 2000s were particularly poisonous to our collective body image. The rise of gossip blogs brought a boom in our obsession with celebrity culture. Magazines were saturated with articles on the ever-shrinking bodies of our favourite starlets and exactly how many almonds they eat to maintain their figure. Red circles of shame were blazoned across the legs and stomachs and arms of any celebrity who failed to look like an airbrushed front cover as they went about their daily life.

The fashion world was still worshipping heroin chic and the diet industry was more shameless than ever, selling us meal plans that revolved around bowls of cereal, juice fasts and cayenne pepper cleanses (which were all just semi-starvation, rebranded). That era was a breeding ground for body hatred and disordered eating – it's miraculous that any of us made it out unscathed (but then again, maybe we didn't). Still, we were not the first generation to be affected by the thin ideal.

Our mothers and grandmothers wanted to be thin, too. Studies have shown that the way mothers talk about bodies, food and weight has a major impact on their daughter's body image and relationship with food.[7] Our mothers are usually our first role models – we look to them as an example, we listen and trust what they say, we mimic the things they do. Our mothers have the power to teach us how to treat ourselves and our bodies based on how they treat their own.

When our mother stands in front of the mirror and picks her reflection to pieces, we learn to look out for the same supposed 'flaws' in ourselves. When our mothers go on crash diets and restrict their eating around us, we learn to monitor our own food intake as well. When our mothers openly criticise how other people look, commenting negatively on the appearance of celebrities or passersby in the street, we learn that body shaming is okay. And when our mothers criticise *us*, our bodies and what we eat, it can be the start of lifelong insecurities.

Even though it's easy to point the finger at our mothers' behaviour and blame them for the damage done to our self-esteem (and absolutely, accountability should be taken), we also have to hold onto enough empathy to realise that they, too, are products of their environment. And most of them were only ever doing as they were taught.

Our mothers grew up in their own era of diet culture and unrealistic body standards – whether it was the inception of Weight Watchers in the 1960s when Twiggy dominated magazine covers, the resurgence of the grapefruit diet in the 1970s when the body ideal was toned, bronzed and busty, or the low-fat-crazed, spandex-clad

1980s. Our mothers, and their mothers, and their mothers before have been conditioned to see bodies and beauty a certain way. And they have passed the lessons down through generations, many of them believing that pursuing thinness isn't only about appearance, but about health, as well.

So much of what we're taught about health and well-being is based on weight before anything else.

The first time I ever defied the authority of a teacher was the day we were lined up in primary school and told that we would all be weighed and measured in order to calculate our BMIs. Supposedly, this would help us find out whether we were healthy. I refused to take part – already hyper-aware that I was larger than my classmates and sure that the shame of having it confirmed would be unbearable.

This was before the UK's National Child Measurement Programme officially launched in 2006, which sees children in reception (ages 4-5) and Year 6 (ages 10-11) weighed and measured once a year in order to collect data on weight trends in children and also advise parents on the BMI category of their child. The Office for Health Improvement and Disparities has continued the programme despite evidence that weighing kids in school can lead to negative mental health outcomes, increased body image issues, and the fact that BMI itself is a flawed, outdated and inaccurate way of measuring an individual's health (especially for children).[8] In the US, approximately half of schools record the BMI of their students.[9]

There are countless public health campaigns that focus solely on weight, and that frame fatness as an individual failing, rather than recognising the complex and varied factors that contribute to someone's body size, plus decades worth of evidence showing that health is far more complicated than weight and weight alone.[10] We are taught that health comes in one size and one size only – no exceptions, no variables. The message is reinforced in our classrooms, by medical professionals, on billboards and on the front pages of newspapers with shocking (misleading) headlines.

Rather than making us healthier, focusing purely on weight and shaming people who fall outside the lines only contributes to weight stigma and pulls focus away from the behavioural *and* societal changes that would lead to better health for all of us. Like improved lessons on nutrition *and* a more regulated food industry. Encouragement to move more *and* better access to community spaces where exercise is possible. Normalised self-care practices *and* funding put into mental health services.

But instead of a holistic, weight-neutral approach to health, all we're told is that fat is bad and thin is good, which fits perfectly with everything else we're shown...

So, when people wonder how little girls get the idea that they need to make their bodies smaller in order to be good enough, all they really need to do is look around at the never-ending number of possible reasons, and take their pick.

* * *

I have made my body smaller many times throughout my life.

I have done all the diets, bought the miracle pills, sweated through boot camps, attended weight-loss groups. I have tried hypnosis, strapped gadgets around my waist, eaten in front of the mirror, weighed myself five times a day.

With each brief attainment of a body closer to the thin ideal, I have waited for the promise of what is supposed to follow: the happiness, the self-love, the days bursting with excitement and opportunity – everything better than it was before.

Each time, without fail, making my body smaller has only ever made my life smaller along with it.

Instead of adventure and spontaneity, there has been monotonous routine: mind-numbingly repetitive work-outs and the same diet-approved foods again and again. The meal plan takes priority over everything – over going out, seeing friends, planning trips, learning new skills. By the time I've hit the goal weight, entire seasons have passed. It took years to realise that life was already happening, and I didn't need to make my body smaller before I was allowed to live it.

Rather than looking in the mirror and finally loving what I saw, there was always another part of my body to zoom in on and find a flaw. There was always another five pounds to lose, another soft part to tone, another bump to smooth. Making our bodies smaller doesn't automatically cure our body image – that has less to do with how we look and more to do with how we've been taught to see ourselves.

As for happiness – the goal that underpins everything that diet culture sells – it was never hiding in the bathroom scales. The inconvenient truth is that no singular end-point ever results in blissful, ever-lasting joy. Happiness isn't hanging on to show itself until after you get promoted, or find a partner, or afford a new car, or lose weight. The *possibility* of happiness is here, in the body you already have – if you allow yourself the chance to feel it.

Making my body smaller never made my life any bigger, and I should have known that it doesn't work that way. Because I'd already seen how small life gets when you chase thinness as far as it can go.

When I was fourteen, I nearly chased thinness straight to my grave. The body hatred and early adoption of dieting from my childhood years latched onto something in my brain and the need to restrict got more and more intense every day. The numbers took over everything, my mind frantically calculating from morning until night.

A voice moved into my head that didn't sound like mine, but she told me exactly what to do: how much food to avoid, how many laps to run, what we needed the scale to say on our next weigh-in. The longer I followed the instructions that my eating disorder gave, the more impossible it felt to do anything else.

When people tried to tell me that I wasn't okay, I didn't believe them. When my clothes started hanging from my frame, I thought they must have gotten bigger in the wash. When I was pulled out of school, I didn't understand what the big deal was. When I was hospitalised, I thought everyone else had it wrong. *I just needed to be smaller.*

But there was no small enough. I couldn't see myself clearly – to this day I have no memory of how my reflection actually looked in the mirror, just a few photographs of a skeletal girl that I don't remember seeing at the time.

The numbers just had to keep going down, that's what the voice said. I had to have more will power, work harder, stay in control. But the feeling of control that an eating disorder offers is only an illusion – once a mental illness is dictating your every decision, you are completely out of control, and the only way to regain some of it, is to start fighting back.

Recovery was the hardest thing I've ever done. I clawed my way through it, railing against every offer of support, relapsing and starting again, so disgusted with my changing body that I covered every mirror in the house. I went back into the world unhealed but desperate to live again, and there it all was: the toxic diet culture, the impossible beauty standards, the normalised disordered eating that was all there before. Just part of everyday life. I sank back into it like a bed made of spikes, and carried on striving for the perfect, thin body.

I didn't stop until years later, when I finally realised that all of it was a lie.

Every promise of what the ideal body brings is just a marketing scheme: a fantasy sold to us by the biggest industries in the world to keep us buying whatever they're selling next.

Every ideal body is just the latest iteration of a man-made standard that changes by the decade – not an undebatable truth about how we all should be.

Every summer spent inside, every night spent hungry, every pay cheque spent on miracle cures, every bit of energy spent counting – all of it was wasted. We could have been doing so much more, if only we hadn't been taught that our ultimate goal in life should be making our bodies small.

I harnessed every bit of rage I could muster on behalf of my younger self, who never should have gone through childhood wishing parts of herself away, and decided that it was time to learn something different. It was time to leave the thin ideal behind, and see how big life could really be.

* * *

It's been ten years since I stopped trying to make my body smaller.

Ten years without going on a diet. Ten years without weighing myself. Ten years of eating intuitively, moving for joy and making peace with this body, however she looks.

I've watched the beauty standard change over time, each new trend bringing a host of treatments and products sold as solutions to our unhappiness. I've seen the diet industry morph into slightly different forms, co-opting the language of wellness, self-love and even body liberation to sell the same old weight-loss plans. I've witnessed how social media has amplified it all: the impossibility of the ideal, the pressure to change ourselves, how easy it is to manipulate images and compare ourselves to what isn't real.

But I've also watched as body positivity has forced its way into mainstream consciousness. I've seen more and more people rejecting diet culture, recognising fatphobia and embracing body neutrality. I've witnessed a rise in representation that I only could have dreamed of before: plus-size main characters with interests outside of losing weight, eating disorder stories that are accurate and sensitively told, thousands of bodies that defy the thin, white, non-disabled, cisgender standard that *used* to be all we got to see. At times, it's felt gloriously hopeful – like the way things always should have been.

Recently though, there have been whispers that we might be going backwards. The current, surgically enhanced standard of beauty seems more prolific than ever and with the increased, widespread use of GLP-1s as a quick-fix weight-loss method, there's been a resurgence of the thin ideal. The headlines have declared that body positivity is over, and thin is back in.

I have watched, bracing myself to witness the damage that will be done to the next generation, knowing that none of this was ever supposed to be a trend.

Our size, the way we look, the way we feel about ourselves are not meant to be dictated by the changing tides of any industry or any power outside of us. Our bodies are not fashion statements or *things* to be remodelled on a whim – they are our homes, each uniquely and perfectly made to their own individual specification.

The idea that we're all supposed to look the same might be the biggest lie of all. Body diversity has existed across all cultures at every point in history. Any standard of how we should be that erases our differences and tells us that there is only one way to be beautiful, happy or good enough is not a standard based in truth or positive intention – and it's definitely not one worth following.

We are the ones who will inhabit these bodies for a lifetime. We get to decide that prioritising our peace within them is more important than whatever trend might come next. After all, trends can only exist if people are willing to follow them.

As for myself, I know that I will never betray my body again in order to fit an ideal that I was never made to fit. This body has carried me through every experience of my life. She has cared for me even when I've mistreated her. She has shown up every day despite what I've put her through. She has loved me even when I have hated her.

Yes, she is bigger and softer than I thought she would be when I used to go to bed dreaming of what we'd look like one day. But she is exactly the way she is meant to be. And I will do my best to accept her at every stage, throughout all her changes, regardless of whatever standard the world is shouting about next.

It's me and her holding onto the peace that we've worked so hard for. That's the new non-negotiable.

ON EATING IN PUBLIC

I'm sitting alone at the back of an afternoon sunlit diner. The air is warm and well spiced from the open kitchen, and all the booths are made of wood. I've ordered sabih: a whole pitta stuffed with aubergine, soft-boiled eggs, chopped fresh vegetables and pickled everything. A pathway of paprika is sprinkled on top and two bowls of sauce are sat alongside; one that looks like golden velvet and the other, deep green with herbs.

I've taken myself for lunch simply because I wanted to. My face is un-made-up and I'm wearing tracksuit bottoms with a pair of well-loved trainers. I looked the waiter in the eye when I walked in and now I'm gazing at my overflowing plate, wondering where to attack first.

I bite. It's heaven.

My body responds with a gentle, *see? I told you we were hungry!,* and I demolish the first half of the pitta without looking up. Sticky sweet-savoury sauce slides down my fingers to my palms and for all I know, my face is covered ... I don't feel even the slightest bit self-conscious. I feel proud because I know exactly what it's taken to get here; to be sat, unapologetically eating in public.

My brain flickers back over a decade of deprivation, of food diaries and morning weigh-ins. Zero-calorie sub-stitutes and suppressed hunger pangs. Rooms filled with shame or praise depending on how much weight I'd lost or gained that week. Nights spent dreaming of running wild in the supermarket without consequence. Days spent burning and earning every bite.

I remember way back, before food and what it could do to my body became something to fear. I remember when eating was okay:

I am five years old and my mum is baking a cake. It's the weekend and these are my favourite days. I'm standing on a stool so that I can see over the counter, and I watch her expertly add the perfect amount of flour, eggs, butter and sugar, a splash of vanilla and a pinch of salt. I wait, eyes wide and taste-buds trembling.

She mixes it all together without needing to check a recipe, and pours the thick, glossy goodness into a waiting baking tin. The best part: she lovingly hands me the whisk, and gives me permission to take it away. I climb down and find a comfortable place to savour my treasure, licking the liquid gold off each spoke as the house fills with the warm scent of sweetness on a Saturday afternoon.

I am six years old and we are visiting my grandparents in their sleepy town where the air smells like salt and we're allowed to stay up later than usual. We've spent the evening at the arcades, sliding copper coins into well-worn slots and praying that a silver claw might deliver us a new fluffy friend. We walk back through the winding streets, past the playground, giddy from being awake at the same time as the street lights.

We wait to be told that it's time for bed, but our bodies are telling us something else: it's been hours since we last ate and we've run our energy stores empty. My

Nan emerges from the kitchen with a plate piled with savoury biscuits and uniform slices of cheese. We sit on the faded carpet and devour our bonus dinner, tired and over-stimulated and completely satisfied.

I am seven years old and summer lasts forever. The days are filled with paintbrushes and Polly Pockets, broken up with pops to the shop or the post office. Every few days our mum disappears for the late afternoon hours, carrying trowels, nets and other grown-up gardening things. We wait for our time to be invited, once her hard work has grown into something we can harvest.

We march up to the communal gardens with buckets in-hand, bouncing with the anticipation of what might be waiting. There, we find rows of carefully tended plants, coming alive with brightly ripe fruit – strawberries, plums and raspberries overflowing. For every berry I place in a punnet, I put another straight in my mouth. We spend the golden hours like this, tongues turning red, bellies full of love.

I have tried to pin down one particular moment when my relationship with food changed, when the joy became shame and the numbers became everything. But it's difficult to point to one molecule of water when you're swimming in an ocean.

Maybe the first droplet came from overheard small talk where certain foods were referred to as 'sinful', 'naughty' or 'bad', as if your ability to resist them determines how good of a person you are. It could have been the TV adverts selling low-fat yoghurt and zero-calorie soft drinks as a way to repent for the sin of indulging your hunger. Or perhaps it was how frequently and casually the idea of burning off whatever you've eaten was mentioned in everyday conversation.

Whatever the first moment was, it was followed by thousands more, ever-present and never questioned. We have grown up within diet culture, and it poisons our relationship with food before we're old enough to even truly understand the impact of the messages we consume. We're left obsessed with what we're eating, hyper-critical of how our bodies look, and filled with shame.

When this is the water we're swimming in, is it any wonder that we carry such complicated feelings when it comes to food?

* * *

When I was eight years old, I had a friend called Erin who I always hoped would invite me over after school. She lived in a terraced house with faded brown carpet and a small fish tank that sat buzzing in the corner of the living room. I'd bring over my fuzzy Sylvanian Family toys and we'd spend hours on the floor building worlds where a small badger and a china doll became best pals, and saved all the other animals from near-constant tornados.

We usually had fish fingers for dinner with some shape of oven-cooked potato. We had a good time by ourselves, but every so often my friend's teenage sister would inexplicably invite us, the children, to hang out with her in her lilac-coloured bedroom, where no conversation was off limits (especially the ones we probably shouldn't have heard).

Of the handful of afternoons spent listening to ghost stories, period worries and who-said-what-about-who-at-school, the conversation I remember in the most vivid detail was about boys, and food, and what girls were supposed to do with both.

"Would you let him use tongues though?" my friend's cousin asked, unashamed. The two older girls sat on the bed while we hovered below, pretending to be invested in our latest Sylvanian natural disaster.

"Euh no, course not," the sister replied, screwing up her face at something I didn't understand.

"You would, wouldn't you!" The cousin clambered across the bed and hit her with a pillow. We'd stopped pretending that we were doing anything other than listening to this brand-new information on tongues and what not to do with them.

"Oi get off! I dunno, we're just like... hanging out," the sister said, as unbothered as she could sound.

"Nah, it's a date. Where are you going?"

"Just to get some food."

"Okay, you can't eat on a date though."

"Yeah..." she trailed off.

Over the next ten minutes, the cousin laid out everything she knew about how to make your date think that you were the perfect girl: *dress nice but not, like, slutty. Shave everything, just in case. Take lip gloss. Don't be desperate. Don't talk about yourself* and *definitely don't eat anything, unless you want him to think you're a cow and get stuff all stuck in your teeth.*

I sat, cross-legged like a little sponge, absorbing. It wasn't the only time I heard the rules about dating and (not) eating whilst growing up – I saw it in magazines, picked it up in sitcoms, watched friends abiding by each rule – but it was the first. And boy, did it stick.

One of my first-ever real dates, at the age of seventeen, involved the terrifying act of eating food.

He was older, twenty-three with a grown-up job and a flat he shared with a roommate. I was meeting him after school and I'd panic-shaved my entire body in the cubicle of a department store toilet after realising I'd left home that morning looking like a teenage girl and not a slippery seal woman. Now, sitting in a booth with a wooden table between me and the man, I was too busy thinking about whether my stomach looked flat whilst sitting down to process any of the words on the menu in front of me.

When he asked what I wanted I went for the smallest, most date-safe option: a chicken wrap, no sides (after all, he had to walk all the way to the tills remembering the order – wouldn't want to weigh him down with my wants).

The evening passed and I listened to him talk about himself while I smiled perfectly at all the most encouraging moments. He gave no indication of whether he found me attractive (we'd only interacted online before the date) and I felt my sweat patches slowly attempting to take over my upper half.

Then, the food arrived. I took bites that a toothless toddler would've laughed at and left half. I couldn't actually tell if I was hungry or not; I was completely detached from my body. It was like I'd left all of my physical needs packed away at home so that I could focus purely on my external appearance and whether he would approve of it.

We left the restaurant and a November evening wind whipped at my bare legs and jacket-less shoulders (the coat didn't go with the 'fit). He asked if I was cold and I said no. I could have been but who knows? I was too busy cursing Mother Nature for blowing my hair away from its assigned place: covering exactly a third of my face.

We went back to his and he asked if I'd like a drink. I said I'd have whatever he was having. He asked my opinion on what film we should watch. I didn't have one. He tentatively and suggestively started to brush my arm with his hand and my brain lit up.

This. This is being wanted. This is why we do everything else.

One half-hearted stroke and it all made sense.

This is why we detach from our hunger.

This is why we learn to have double-vision: one view looking out at the world and the other always perceiving how the world is looking at us.

This is why we sweat, and tweeze, and cry, and swallow down, and buy and buy and buy.

Being wanted – having our desirability validated – is where we've been taught to find our worth since forever. *And fuck me, it feels good.*

It feels like being told we got the answer right before anyone else. Like finding a flavour that reminds you of being young and in a foreign country and full of wonder. Like time doesn't exist. It feels like everything might be okay.

And we can have that – the being wanted – as long as we're willing to play by the rules; as long as we're willing to be perfect...

It hits me, back in the diner (in my thirty-year-old body and brain) that the real reason why 'perfect' women don't eat in public has little to do with sticky fingers or salad stuck in teeth. But because perfect women don't have needs.

Perfect women, as defined by patriarchal standards, are hollow. They don't need to order a side of garlic bread. They don't need a coat even when it's four degrees outside. They don't need to voice their discomfort when they hear a questionable opinion. They don't need emotional reassurance when something feels off. They don't need to come when you have sex and they don't need anything from you after. They don't *need*. So if we want to be perfect, we learn to leave our needs at home and turn up, hollow, ready to be the version of 'woman' we've been primed to be since we sat in our friend's sister's bedroom, listening to *the rules* for the very first time. Hoping that if we play the game right, we'll be wanted. And then everything might be okay...

The morning after that first date I did my part, as rehearsed. I salvaged my make-up in the early light of the bathroom mirror down the hall. I freshened up my 'pits and baby wiped my lips. I slid, seal-like back into bed and positioned myself to appear as desirable as possible for when the man next to me woke up.

I secured another hit of validation – though it was both sleepier and starker in the daylight. And when he was done, he started watching YouTube videos on his phone and asking me what time my train left. There was no being wanted left. I'd exhausted the resource.

I made my way to the station, trying to harness a feeling of empowerment but coming up against every other feeling I'd ignored for the past twenty-four hours.

I got to the platform, and my needs came flooding back. I was starving. I was tired. My bra was uncomfortable. I was cold. I found a vending machine and bought a chocolate bar, got on the train and sat huddled in a corner, inhaling the calories my body so desperately needed. The caramel was sweeter than any I'd ever tasted and the nougat felt heaven-sent. I glanced around to check nobody had seen me, eating in public so brazenly.

I played this game for years, following the rules of 'perfect' womanhood passed down to me and abandoning myself for fleeting moments of feeling wanted by someone else. Years of hunger, discomfort, suppressing my voice and hiding my human bodily needs. And it worked, for a while.

But the hits became less and less thrilling. The performance had started to exhaust me.

I reached a point where I no longer wanted to sacrifice my true self for the sake of desirability. And I realised, somewhere along the way, that the type of validation that requires you to hollow yourself out in order to secure it, isn't worth having at all.

Ten years after that first date, I found myself on another, with a different man, in the same place.

I was wearing an outfit that I could breathe in, and when I sat across from him in that wooden booth, I didn't worry about whether my stomach looked flat sitting down. I was hungry, so I ordered exactly what I wanted: a burger, two sides and a drink. And I ate. I ate without apology or shame, because there is no room for either of those things when it comes to our human needs.

He talked about himself a lot and we disagreed on a few things. I allowed myself to wonder whether I liked him, rather than simply focusing on securing his attraction to me. I didn't try to angle myself into the most visually appealing positions. I didn't apologise for the light sweat that gathered along my forehead. I did not shrink under his gaze and I did not perform. I was not perfect, and for the first time, I didn't care.

I left the date without the validation of being wanted; I didn't want him either so that was fine. But my belly was full. I was tucked warmly into my favourite coat. I hadn't abandoned myself, even when the urge to perform had flickered in me like muscle memory. And the feeling of refusing to make myself small felt like a whole new kind of validation.

It wasn't quite as electric or intoxicating as those first hits all those years ago, but it felt solid. It was mine, I had fought for it and nobody could take it from me. Not even a man who didn't want to fuck me or a culture built on teaching women to hate what makes us whole. Nobody else gets a say. I don't need their want because I want myself, with all of my needs, all of my undesirable, all of my imperfect.

And fuck me, it feels good.

It feels like being told you've got the answer right before anyone else. Like finding a flavour that reminds you of being young and in a foreign country and full of wonder. Like time doesn't exist. It feels like everything might be okay.

Except now, I know that 'okay' doesn't depend on me showing up as anyone other than entirely who I am, and enjoying every single bite.

* * *

In the diner, I've finished my meal and I allow myself to sit back in a position that generations of women before me would have called 'unladylike'.

A few flavours are still dancing on my tongue and I take a moment to check in with my body. *What do I need, now? Has my hunger been fully satiated? Am I thirsty? Do I want anything else?*

There's a freshly baked cinnamon loaf on a counter in front of me and my tastebuds perk up at the thought of it. My stomach tells me that we're full, so I decide to take a slice for the road – no rush, no need to eat past the point of fullness, there is no crash diet waiting around the corner pressuring us to binge while we can.

I remember the years coloured with deep shame at the thought of ordering a dessert. If we *had* to eat in public, there was no way we'd be caught enjoying the kind of food that diet culture had taught us to place in the 'bad' category. That shame is so often amplified for anyone who exists in a larger body, since fatphobic narratives around health lead us to believe that what bigger people eat should be open to public opinion.

I pay and leave the restaurant, floating on the novelty of enjoying my own company after thinking for so long that doing things alone was a social failing. I walk home the long way, noticing the rust in the leaves and picturing the kind of people who live in the houses on this street.

Me, my body, my feelings and my needs are more connected than they have ever been. And we never could have gotten here, if we carried on believing that we weren't allowed to eat.

MOVEMENT

When I was young, I would fling my body through space as if every shape I made was magic. I would float my limbs through uncoordinated sequences and feel like I was the sea herself. I would cut through the air, feet ricocheting off the grass so fast that if I jumped, I *knew* I would float above it.

I think those moments are still the closest thing to euphoria that I've ever experienced. When I close my eyes in my adult body and picture the days when I've been genuinely happiest, the memories are always filled with joyful movement and carefree connection to my body.

Our bodies remember how it once felt to move without the weighted opinions of the world. To try a new activity, be bad at it and enjoy it anyway! To splash around a pool, only invested in which friends were mermaids and who could do a handstand underwater. To dance around a bedroom and feel like a popstar, wearing pyjamas and getting every move wrong.

We were once so connected to the wonder of moving our bodies, not as a means to an end or something to tick off the list. We moved because moving was the best thing we could do, jumping and playing, our bodies folding and bending in ways we weren't even paying attention to.

We hadn't been taught to think about that yet – the way we might look to others while we were chasing after our own joy. We hadn't yet read the magazine articles telling us the best ways to move to make parts of ourselves smaller. We hadn't yet learned that movement was a way to punish ourselves, to make up for things, to bargain for our next meal.

But we get older. Diet culture permeates our innocence. Opinions come. And one by one, we absorb them.

We get the message that some types of movement are only worth doing if we're good at them. We stop dancing unless we are dancers. We stop running unless we are runners. We stop being encouraged to pursue any kind of competitive sport unless there's a chance we will win. We notice that the people who are celebrated for the way they move are also – and often even more so – celebrated for the way they look.

At some point, we're shamed for our size or shape, how we sweat or the body hair that's showing while we're outside. Maybe we're told that girls don't play football or boys don't take dance lessons. If we belong to communities of colour, we might be warned to get out of the sun before our skin gets any darker.

Over time, something shifts in our minds when it comes to movement: joy isn't the priority, having fun isn't the goal.

Rather than being in our bodies – focused on the feeling of blood pumping, lungs expanding, muscles working in rhythm – we have (without our permission) a TV screen installed in our minds. On it, we see ourselves exactly as the world must see us.

For some of us, that screen never turns off.

It shows us that when we run, the fleshy parts of our body bounce freely along with us. But, according to the rules of the 'ideal' body, this is wrong. So, we apologise by sucking ourselves in, stunting our breath, shrinking ourselves and moving only in controlled ways.

The screen points out that we look nothing like the professional dancers from the video when we let our bodies move to music. We adjust our posture, minimise our movements and think about every angle we're being perceived from.

The screen zooms in on the droplets of sweat that gather innocently around our face while we're playing a game outside. We decide to be less enthusiastic, wear more make-up or not play the next time we're asked.

We move as if we're getting something wrong with every step, avoid exerting ourselves more than necessary, and dread anything that leaves us visibly out of breath. Movement used to feel like the best part of having a body, and slowly, that connection is taken away. In its place we grow shame, hypervigilance, and apology stacked on apology. We follow the rules and the joy of movement disappears, without us even realising what we've lost.

For a long time, every move my body made was a bargaining chip: *if I can keep going for this long, will it show on the morning weigh-in? If I do this many reps, will it give me a stomach like hers? If I punish myself today, will it bring me a body that might be worth something more than punishment tomorrow?*

Every step was calculated and logged. Every day was a chance to do more.

I turned down invitations that clashed with my workout schedule. I got knots and twists and aches and ignored them all. I spent hours repeating the same movements, thinking about nothing but how I would look after another month of forcing myself through. I stripped all of the joy from movement so that one day, hopefully, I might be able to move through the world in a body that felt good enough.

It is heartbreaking the way we believe that harming ourselves will lead to us being happy.

Eventually, inevitably, the regime always cracked. It turns out that forcing yourself to do things you hate for an impossible end goal isn't sustainable, no matter how much the concept of will power has been drilled into your brain.

And when I finally started to heal from all the damage that diet culture had done, there was a reckoning to be had. First, with stillness. With allowing what I had demonised and feared for so long: letting myself be still.

In the stillness, I had no choice but to be honest with myself about how toxic my relationship with movement had become. I let my muscles rest. I fuelled my body without needing to use up every bite of energy. For the first time in years, I was not burning, not counting, not bargaining – simply being.

And after being still for long enough to drain the worst of diet culture's poison, it was time to start from scratch. Re-introduce myself to movement, like a relationship gone toxic resetting to strangers. It was time to get to know movement as it always should have been: freeing, joyful, alive.

I started with walking. Passing by leaves and bended trees, training my brain to think about the beauty of the day instead of whether I could feel my stomach swaying. I took deep, generous breaths and with every exhale filled my mind with nothing but "be here, be here, be here".

I passed by strangers and refused to switch on that old TV screen to see what they saw when they looked at me. What about what I saw? What about how I felt? What about: this body belongs to me, no need for anyone else's approval to validate her being.

When I reacquainted myself with movement again, it was time to try something new. I landed on yoga, knowing that I didn't understand the poses, the names, and that I was going to look different to the lean, supple teachers I was learning from. I wasn't very flexible, but I did it anyway. I couldn't hold the poses for long, but I tried. I wasn't familiar with breathwork, but I gave it a go.

There were so many kinds of movement that I'd been hoarding preconceptions about. I thought I had to look a certain way or be at a certain skill level before I could even try. How limiting is that? Needing to look perfect and be great before you've even tried something?

What about the people who aren't great, but are having a great fucking time? What about the people who aren't trying to be athletes but still want the warmth of endorphins, of having teammates, of trying something new? Can we get some recognition for the people who don't know what they're doing, but choose to move their body anyway?

Not knowing the names of yoga poses won't stop you from feeling the effects of the stretch. Not being the best in the class won't stop the joyful explosion of happy chemicals releasing in your brain. Not looking the same as everyone else won't stop you, unless you let it.

Recently I started challenging myself to go to a dance class that is way out of my comfort zone. I lag behind, I forget the moves, I sweat in bucketloads. And at the same time, I am so filled with joy.

I've even rediscovered the joy of movement in places that I thought had been burned beyond repair. When my relationship with exercise was at its most toxic, running was a non-negotiable. It had to be done every day for X amount of minutes at X speed. No excuses. No breaks. No time off for injury or illness.

When the healing began, I put myself on a running ban. I vowed to stop moving my body in ways I'd used to harm myself until I could go back with a different mindset. First there was the walking, then there was the yoga, and the dancing came back too. But running? I just couldn't associate it with anything other than punishment.

Then one day, long enough later for all the cells in my body to be different to what they once were, I went for a walk. I was in a different city, with a different life. I had moved far from the girl who was all hunger and spikes. And that day, somewhere from inside my body, a little spring pushed me forwards.

I started to jog, clothes flapping and belly bouncing as I went. My breathing got quicker and the rhythm of that breath in time with my feet hitting the ground felt almost like a meditation. It got hard, but I wanted to keep going. It got too hard, so I had a break. Then I picked it up again. As I rounded the corner onto the final stretch before home, I let my legs break out into a sprint.

Buildings rushed past me. My arms sliced through the air. It felt like I was leaping for miles with every stride. And just then, my body remembered: *we used to love this.* Back when we were young and every field was filled with the possibility of play. Remember how free we used to feel? Remember how fast we could go? Remember how sure we were that if we jumped, we could start floating above it all?

I slowed myself to stop outside my door just in time for a few tears to arrive. We'd done it! We'd finally taken back another thing that had been tainted for so long. I felt overwhelmed with endorphins, with pride, but most of all I just felt... happy.

In that moment, I had reclaimed something that a younger version of me did every day simply because she loved it. I had connected brain to body, body to spirit, shook off shame and taken back something that has *always* been mine.

Finally, I remembered: moving is one of the best parts about having a body. And I won't let diet culture take that away from me ever again.

THE PRETTY TAX

Starting from the age of twelve, I refused to open the front door unless I had my make-up on. It didn't matter whether it was the postman or a friend stopping by unexpectedly, the knocks would be ignored. I would freeze and hide around the corner from the door, holding my breath and feeling my body burn with anxiety until they'd left.

What if they'd seen me through the blurred glass?! What if I'd been perceived in my natural state?! I had a zero-tolerance policy on letting outsiders see how I actually looked. As if I'd committed a crime by looking like a human girl rather than an airbrushed supermodel as I went about my Tuesday morning.

When I *did* go out into the world, how I looked to others was all I ever thought about. I'd go to the cinema with one set of eyes on the screen and another set noticing if anyone glanced in my direction. I'd get on a train and choose my seat based on what I believed was my best side, then spend the journey upright, perfectly poised, alert to every person who entered the carriage.

Being visually appealing was the price I believed I had to pay in order to exist in public. As if some patriarchal gatekeeper had set up shop outside my house to tax me the price of pretty every time I wanted to leave.

And the rules of 'pretty' were always painfully specific. Every hair in the perfect place. Every pore perfectly covered. Every lash perfectly coated. Every line perfectly drawn. Make some things smaller and some things bigger and some things invisible altogether. And before you get any ideas – none of this is based on what feels creative or fun or even remotely authentic to you. These are simply the rules passed down from the ever-changing beauty standard; follow them exactly, or spend your days feeling unworthy.

I learned how to pay the tax, picking up tips and tricks on the endless ways I could be prettier than I was before. A magazine told me which shade of eyeshadow to wear to make my eyes look the most seductive. A YouTube tutorial showed me how to contour my jaw to hide my double chin. A celebrity shared the secret to her shiny, volumised hair and I bought whatever she was selling.

At its most expensive, the price of the pretty tax meant waking up two hours early to paint and style myself before every school day. It meant finding a mirror once an hour to re-apply and reset. It meant monitoring every expression, every movement, every angle to make sure nothing was ruining the prettiness I was working so hard to perform.

At the end of those days, I was exhausted. After the energy poured into creating the illusion, plus the effort to keep it all in place, there was the hyper-awareness of everyone's gaze, and a never-ending analysis of whether they thought I was pretty enough. That kind of constant projection of what everyone around you is thinking about how you look takes up as much brain space as a full-time job. Still, I never dared to entertain the possibility of refusing to pay the tax – that simply didn't feel like an option.

We pour so many resources into paying the pretty tax because we believe (we're taught) that when we do, we become worthy of being seen. Only when we disguise our 'flaws' can we transform into our *best* selves – and it's only our best self that should be witnessed in the world. If we are daring to take up space, the *least* we can do is be aesthetically pleasing, placate the male gaze, and pay the tax.

And let's be clear: in a lot of ways, our efforts will be rewarded. Those of us who pass the threshold of being pretty *enough* will be awarded a range of privileges – more access, more opportunity, more kindness from anyone who believes that a woman's appearance is what she should be judged by. But at what cost?

For every few who can morph themselves close enough to the beauty standard to reap the rewards, there are hundreds more obsessively striving for a goal that's constantly changing to become less and less attainable to the majority. And all of us, no matter how much pretty privilege we can acquire, are harmed in the end. We all sacrifice so much of our time, energy, money and self-worth reaching for pretty *enough*.

Paying the pretty tax steals our ability to be truly present wherever we are. When we are so hyper-focused on how we look to everyone around us, we don't get to take up that space and really be in it – absorbing our surroundings, letting life flow through our senses, being in the moment. We exist more as ornaments for other people's viewing than as participating, fully-rounded members of the world.

Ultimately, the pretty tax is not just about how we look. It's about how much of our energy we're willing to trade to prove that we deserve our place.

* * *

By the time I realised the price I was really paying, I was twenty-one and terrified of what it might mean to leave it all behind – to reject the beauty standard, redefine my value on my own terms and dare to take up space as my natural self. But something in me knew that it was a fear worth pushing through; that there could be a sense of freedom on the other side that I'd never felt before.

I channelled all the feminist rage I could muster and challenged myself to stop wearing make-up. I chopped off my hair; the long golden-brown waves that I always spent hours perfecting turned into a short, unstyled bob. I stopped choosing my clothing based solely on which outfit would make me appear the smallest. I dared myself to go out into the world and de-programme the conditioning that told me to focus primarily on how I looked to other people. I gave myself permission to look out at the world, instead.

It might not have seemed like a big deal to anyone else. I was still a young, slim, able-bodied woman with a reasonable amount of natural pretty privilege. But to me it was huge. It was an uncloaking of my real self after so many years of hiding. It was a reclaiming of all the authority I'd given to other people to validate my presence. And it was the start of seeing myself, and the world, completely differently.

After I stopped paying the pretty tax, I couldn't help but notice every piece of cultural conditioning working to make us believe that we aren't worthy of being seen as we are. I noticed that every women's magazine cover featured a celebrity who'd either been airbrushed beyond recognition, or had dared to 'let herself go' and found herself subject to a bright red circle of shame.

I saw the ways that advertisers shamelessly called our faces tired and our hair lifeless, and how every week a new product promised to change our lives: a mascara that would finally make them notice us, a face cream that would help us look twenty years younger. Cosmetic surgery was increasingly popular but also still taboo, meaning that most of our beauty idols wouldn't admit to having work done as they sold us the latest solution to supposedly help us look like them.

I was suddenly aware of how many apologies left the lips of women around me every day for nothing more than how they looked. *Sorry about my face, I didn't have time to put on make-up. Sorry my hair isn't done, it's not normally like this. Sorry I look so tired, it's been a long week. Sorry, sorry, sorry...*

The amount we all apologise for simply existing in our own skin is a testament to how deeply we've been conditioned to see our appearance as the most important thing we have to offer.

Every time I noticed another piece of messaging encouraging us to feel ashamed of how we look, I got angrier and angrier. None of us asked for this. None of us willingly chose to grow up within a culture that would reduce our worth to how well we can emulate an exclusionary and unrealistic beauty standard. Why hasn't this been dismantled already?

No doubt the reason has something to do with the roughly £450 billion in revenue that the beauty industry made worldwide in 2023, a number that's projected to grow year by year. Wherever women can be taught to carry shame about a natural part of themselves, there is profit to be made. As Dr. Gail Dines famously said, "If tomorrow, women woke up and decided they really liked their bodies, just think how many industries would go out of business."

I decided that my self-esteem was worth more than any amount of money an industry could make from convincing me to hate the way I look. I wasn't buying it anymore.

The intense discomfort that followed me around for the first couple of weeks as I tried to unlearn all of those old lessons gradually started to ease. I caught myself when I felt the need to suck in my stomach or reposition my hair as somebody walked by. I fought the urge to zoom in on my reflection in every mirror I passed. I started to feel less and less apologetic about showing up exactly as I was, whether I was going to the supermarket or a social event.

After a few months, I felt like a different person. I couldn't believe I'd spent so many years convinced that I was unworthy of being in the world unless I looked a certain way. I was worthy of being anywhere I wanted to be! And I didn't need to validate my presence by fitting into a standard that I never signed up for in the first place.

One day, as I was running errands around town in an outfit I would've deemed too unflattering to wear in public before, a splash of colour caught the corner of my eye. I turned and saw a person dressed in every shade you could imagine. They had short, purple hair styled into spikes, a dress bursting with oranges and yellows, emerald green tights and chunky turquoise shoes. They bounced around with more confidence than I'd ever witnessed in one person; clattering with rainbow bangles and smiling through lips lined in the brightest possible pink.

I realised then that refusing to pay the pretty tax didn't have to mean abandoning self-decoration altogether. This person clearly wasn't interested in fitting into the societally accepted beauty standard, but still they adorned themselves head-to-toe. They surely spent hours focusing on their appearance before stepping out of the house, but they weren't paying the pretty tax in the way that so many of us do. They were doing it for themselves. Expressing some part of who they were with how they looked, making their own rules, setting their own standard.

I went home and started to question whether there were any parts of my old beauty routine that I missed. I didn't miss the pressure of feeling like I *had* to paint my face before I could be seen, but I did recognise how meditative putting my make-up on could sometimes be. And when I allowed myself to experiment with different colours and techniques, it became a form of creativity, too.

I didn't want to go back to using my hair as a shield to hide my face behind on the days I didn't feel pretty enough, but I liked the idea of using it as a form of decoration. And I'd always wondered how it might feel to dye it an unexpected colour: unicorn shades of blue and lilac, maybe even a bright pink...

I decided to allow some focus on aesthetics back into my life, on my own terms. I knew that I would never reduce my worth to how well I fit into a narrow set of beauty standards ever again, which meant that I was free to explore how I might adorn myself when I was making decisions that were truly for me, and nobody else. Starting with buying myself a brand-new lipstick, in the brightest shade of pink I could find.

* * *

Dismantling the pretty tax is not necessarily a black-and-white process.

Some days I imagine what it would be like to exist in a society where all the energy we pour into appearance gets collected up and redistributed into things like caring for others, finding world-saving solutions and making more art. A part of me believes that the answer is for us to collectively refuse to focus on how we look altogether.

Other days, I still spend an hour painting my face, and I enjoy it. I stare into my wardrobe and let the colours wash over me until I land on exactly how I want to feel when I step outside. I pay someone to draw intricate designs on my fingernails that match the shades I've dyed my hair. I love colour. I love adornment. I love expression.

I think a lot of us are holding beliefs about beauty that feel contradictory. We so badly want to be seen as more than how we look but how we look is still something that we think about every day. We believe *in theory* that appearance isn't important, but it still feels important when we're trying to figure out which version of ourselves to present to the world. We want to not care, but society constantly reminds us that we have to.

We also beat ourselves up for holding both beliefs, and those of us who identify as feminists feel like we're betraying the cause in some way.

Being aware of our contradictions and reflecting on how we can exist in a way that's more aligned with our values is a good thing – it's how we grow. But I wish we could hold that awareness in a way that also allows some grace towards ourselves and the world we're currently navigating.

Yes, we are more than our physical selves. And we still exist in a world where the physical is unignorable.

Yes, we deserve to take up space regardless of how we show up. And a lot of spaces will still reward the people who can show up in certain ways, and restrict access to others who can't.

Yes, we should know that we are good enough regardless of how we look. And we've been conditioned since birth to place our value on our reflection and unlearning that, within a culture that still upholds and perpetuates the same lessons, is a long and difficult journey that looks different to everybody.

Dismantling the pretty tax does not have to be an all-or-nothing negotiation. We shouldn't be aiming to get rid of the shame that the beauty standard has taught us, only to replace it with the shame of not rejecting it completely enough. We don't need to feel bad on top of feeling bad. What we need is the freedom to decide for ourselves.

Some of us will refuse to pay the pretty tax by banishing all focus on aesthetics. We'll feel the freest when we don't give a single fuck about how we look. We'll take back every bit of time we used to spend on our outsides and fill ourselves from the inside instead. And that will be beautiful.

Some of us will choose to leave the house with a full face of make-up, strutting in a ballgown and heels and still refuse to pay the pretty tax. We will adorn our bodies in ways that affirm *our* taste, before anyone else's. We will channel our creativity and turn ourselves into art. We will know we are worthy of being present wherever we go. And that will be beautiful.

A lot of us will land somewhere in the middle. We will do our best to question why we feel the need to look a certain way. Some days we will find the strength to go against that pressure, but we won't want every day to feel like a battle. Some of our decisions will feel empowering. Others will just be what we've always known. We will try. And that will be beautiful.

There is no uniform guide to opening our front doors and evicting the patriarchal gatekeeper set up to charge us the pretty tax. It will be up to each of us to explore our options, to be honest with ourselves, to think critically about the choices we're making and to choose ourselves first.

The choice of how we present ourselves should start and finish with us. Nobody else's gaze should hold the power to validate our existence in the world.

We are entitled to the space we take up simply because *we are*. We exist in public and therefore we deserve to be in public.

We are allowed to explore, to connect, to absorb the world whether we are in our most natural form or our most decorated.

We have the right to be dressed-up or not, to wear colour or not, to put on lipstick or not. We deserve to move unapologetically through crowds, sway freely on dance-floors, hold stages and walk home safely. We are entitled to be, in any state, without apology. We are entitled to so much that we were never told to expect and it starts with the space we take up.

It starts with knowing that our right to exist as we are isn't earned, it's owed – no conditions, no requirements, no price to pay.

WHAT NATURALLY GROWS

I was first introduced to my armpit hair at the age of twenty-eight.

Like a lot of us, I'd started shaving them before there was really anything there, and I just... didn't stop. The razor would come out before a night out, every morning of a summer's day, every time there was a chance that another person might see my body.

It never felt optional: getting rid of whatever decided to sprout from my skin anywhere from the eyebrows down. Body hair was unhygienic, unfeminine, unattractive, unacceptable. I'd learned that lesson from every billboard, every runway and every Hollywood rom-com. Beautiful women are hairless, poreless, smooth and tight. Our bodies should not be an untended wilderness left to its own devices, they should be preened and polished and never changing!

I was so aware of this truth that I studied my skin for years in the run-up to anything growing from it. Once I'd turned ten, and the blue and white chequered dresses came out for the spring term of primary school, I spent every morning scanning my legs for signs of something untamed. I'd heard horror stories of girls who suddenly grew tufts overnight and went to school the next day unprepared for the changing-room shame. That was *not* going to be me. I would monitor every square inch of myself so that I was ready to pounce at the first sign of the wild beast of my body breaking free.

And one day, they appeared. A few golden hairs softly sprawling across my shins. I crept to the bathroom, reached for the razor my dad used to shave his face, and dry-shaved the first few layers of my skin off along with those harmless little hairs. A smattering of blood and a short lesson on how to shave safely (especially around the ankles!) later, and I was off!

Every shower came to include a full body shave. The hairs never made it past the stubble stage before being forcefully removed. In fact, forceful removal was a technique I applied to most of the things my body tried to grow that fell outside of the prescribed beauty standard. Body fat could be ruthlessly burned away. Cellulite could be scrubbed into oblivion. Once I had the funds and I was old enough, I could pay to literally have parts of myself chopped off and reformed. I made lists of everything I was going to change. I would tame it all.

Rather than recognising my body as an ever-evolving animal that gave me a home and a way to experience the world, I only ever saw her as something to get under control. Something to work on. Something to make less of. As women, we're taught to start disappearing ourselves as soon as we come to be.

I don't feel like I can write about body hair without also writing about men – my relationship to both is inextricably linked. It was a boy who first pointed out the hairs growing on my upper lip that I went home and shaved for years after. It was a boy who told me that he wouldn't have sex with any girl unless she was shaved clean. It is men who have had the strongest opinions, the most disgust in their voices when speaking about hairy women. All the while sprouting shamelessly from every pore.

What makes us 'dirty' and 'unhygienic' doesn't apply to them. What counts as evidence that we've let ourselves go is unremarkable on their bodies. What we spend hours and thousands eradicating from our skin is something they're encouraged to embrace. Not because there is some major biological difference between our hairs and theirs, but just because those are the rules.

It was rooms of men who first realised the profit potential of teaching women that hairlessness and femininity go hand in hand. It was men who invented slogans telling women that the way to avoid embarrassment was to make sure they were hair-free. One 1922 magazine ad for Ashes of Roses hair removal cream starts with the line "The fastidious woman of today must have immaculate underarms if she is to be unembarrassed."[11] And 'immaculate' obviously means bare.

Throughout history, there has been infinitely more focus on women's body hair than on men's. Our hair has been symbolic of our sexual habits, has been used to show differences in class, and has even been linked to patriotism. When women in the US were subject to a shortage of stockings during World War II due to nylon supplies being put towards war efforts, ditching the tights and picking up a new Gillette razor to keep legs smooth was a beauty standard that also showed support for the troops!

Our current cultural disdain for body hair no doubt also has a racialised component. European naturalists of the eighteenth and nineteenth centuries studied physiological differences across races in order to find evidence justifying the superiority of the white race. They argued that people of colour were less evolved, and pointed to their body hair as evidence of them being a primitive species. Once body hair was associated with racial inferiority, it was even easier to convince white women that they had to be hair-free. As Rebecca Herzig quotes in her book *Plucked: A History of Hair Removal,* removing body hair was a way to "separate oneself from cruder people, the lower class and immigrant."[12]

Wherever you look to find answers to the question of why women feel the way they do about their body hair, you will find men. They're setting the standard, dishing out shame, raking in the profit, dictating how we should change ourselves to fit their preferences. If I'm being entirely honest with myself, it was men who I was shaving for. To avoid their judgement and gain their approval. To prove my desirability and show that I was playing by the rules.

Being hairless is a clear, visible marker that you have understood what's expected of you as a woman, and to some extent, you're willing to comply. That's why a hairy woman is so alarming to a patriarchal man – not because of the hair itself (which they're used to seeing on their own body every day) – but because the hair is a broken agreement. The hair says, "I know what is expected of me, and I won't do it." The hair is a rebellion, and a threat to the order of things. If a woman is choosing to

the shadows under my arms, raised his bushy eyebrows and said, "What's this?"

"What does it look like?" I replied casually, having practised the conversation in my mind ten times already.

"Well, I know what it is, I mean why's it there?" he fumbled.

"My body grows hair there, doesn't yours?"

"Yeah but... why haven't you shaved it?"

"I just haven't," I said, my resolve beginning to waver with the disgust creeping onto his face.

"Alright then." He got up from the bed, leaving me to sit with the broken agreements all over my body.

I shaved soon after. I kept cutting off parts of myself to make that relationship work until I barely recognised what was left.

It was a Sunday morning when I decided to stop. I'd moved through the heaviest parts of heartbreak: the days when everything hurts and nobody understands and why couldn't it have just gone differently? I'd hidden away and watched fifteen seasons of a show I'd never heard of before, decided I hated my whole wardrobe (everything felt attached to him), let my body run wild and some days unwashed and finally, after weeks, I'd emerged ready to clean myself off and re-enter the world.

I got into the shower and instinctively reached out for my razor. In the time that I'd been grieving, I'd grown a layer of protective fuzz in all the places hair wasn't allowed to be. As if my body had given me some extra padding to weather what felt like an unbearable storm.

As my fingers wrapped around the plastic handle that carried the blade, something pulled at my heart. How could I keep getting rid of a part of myself that my body, with all her evolutionary wisdom, all of her resilience, all of her love for me, had intentionally continued to grow?

How could I continue to shave, when it was never truly for me in the first place?

It struck me that I was nearing the end of my third decade, and I'd never even met this part of myself. Had never even given her a chance to grow to her full potential. Had always just cut, stripped, waxed, burned, melted away before she had a chance to see daylight.

I couldn't do it anymore. I couldn't destroy what naturally grows.

My brain buzzed with all the men who would think I was disgusting. All the dates I wouldn't have. All the train journeys where I'd feel self-conscious. All the women who've soaked in their patriarchal conditioning so well that they're willing to do the devil's work for him and shame other women for transgressing the rules. All the family members who won't get it. All the strangers on the internet who'll have something to say.

I decided to choose myself above them all. I decided to choose my comfort, my exploration, my freedom, my growth above everything.

Let them be disgusted. Let them not understand. Any person who hasn't engaged in enough critical thinking to realise that other people's bodies aren't their business isn't my type of person anyway. Let what my body grows be a shortcut to finding out who they really are.

I left the shower with my wild, untamed hair, and did the same every day until my razor started to rust. I started to feel a little rush of joy at letting my body do whatever she naturally wanted to. I watched as patterns formed in the direction of my hairs and spent moments gently stroking my new soft parts as I watched TV or read a book. I went outside, lifted my arms and bared my legs and didn't look down regardless of who I sensed had noticed.

When I move through the world and people catch a glimpse of my body hair, I watch their faces travel through a series of emotions before it decides where to settle. I've seen people land on discomfort. I've seen people land on disgust. I've seen people turn to the person next to them with their mouths hanging open in shock. But for the most part, I see people land on indifference; they don't know me and I don't know them, and after this brief crossing of our paths, my body will likely never enter their consciousness again.

Regardless of reactions, opinions, projections, I still choose myself above it all. And I haven't regretted it yet.

Deciding not to shave anymore isn't a world-changing revolution. There are women all over the world rebelling against patriarchal standards in far more radical ways.

But it's another small reclamation. A permission to my body to be as she is. An offering to my younger self whose every decision was guided by shame. We will do our best to keep learning something different, and to proudly call this wild place home.

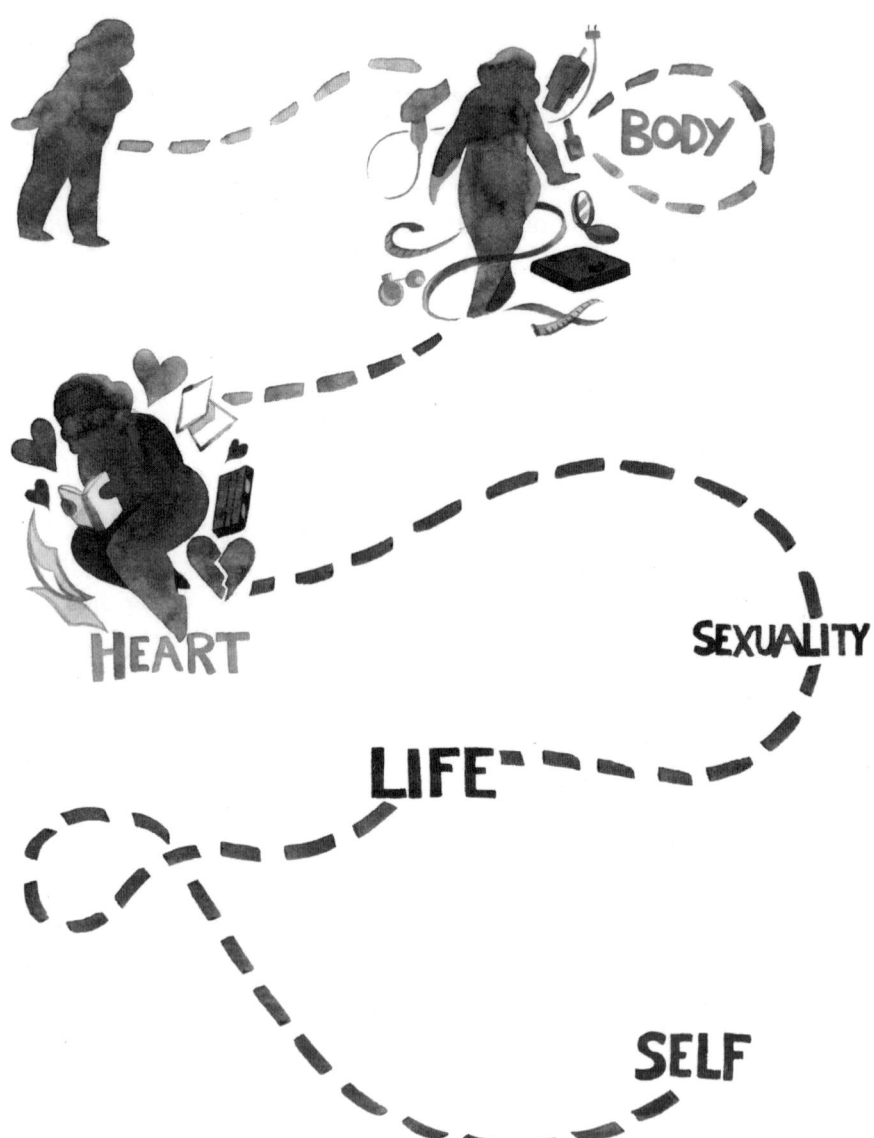

HEART

they tell you that love is all these things,
the books, the songs, the dreams
pass you the outline with only
half a smile
giving away crashes
they've already seen
you gaze through days
holding the stencil to your eye
hunger bleeding into all you see.
so when a shape appears that
threatens to fit
reality is a wild thing
and your wanting: shears.
they tell you that love is all these things,
and they believe what they're saying
to be true.
but if we saw young hearts as gold
we'd protect them with warning, too.
for every stumbling miracle
for every floating high
for every youth sprung vision
and theft from yours to mine
here is another stencil

perhaps more important than the first
listen tenderly, soft one.
this is what love is not:
Love is not feeling danger, and shaking off how you
were raised.
Love is not losing time and space and yourself and
days and days.
Love is not sitting across a table while they tell you
with words that you're enough.
Love is not sitting alone at night while they show you
with actions that you are not.
Love is not learning how to weather storms.
    Love is not performing to be held.
Love is not giving until you have nothing left while they
think of nothing but themselves.
Love is not having to cover your ears.
Love is not dancing on spikes.
Love is not ignoring your knowing while you're forced
to lie to everyone in your life.
Love is not being thankful that they saved you, when
they were the one who pushed you off the edge.
Love is not feeling more and more like yourself every
time they left.
Love doesn't leave you the way that they did: barely
recognising yourself. Love should make you big
instead of small. Love makes you more, not less.
it's okay, soft one. You're here now. I promise that You
are Yours.
You know. deeply know. carry Your knowing
forwards.
no need to walk around with the stencil held to Your
eye. open Yourself to the world. Be brave and
curious and honest. Reclaim Your own life.

they tell You that love is all these things,
and perhaps for themselves, they were right.
but You, knowing one, have ink pressed from
   crushed hearts.
rewrite, rewrite, rewrite.

WHEN IT'S TIME TO LEAVE

"I didn't think you were the type of woman who would stay..." he said casually from across the table, fork rifling through a bowl of fresh leaves while a waiter hovered a few feet away.

He said it with the carefree tone of someone who has no idea that they'd just run a spear through one of my deepest insecurities. I felt physically repelled from the room.

I'd just finished telling the friend (who I hadn't seen in a while) what had really happened in my last relationship and why I'd finally ended it. From his perspective we'd been obnoxiously happy together; seemingly perfect for each other. He listened with his eyebrows raised as I shared the reality.

I'd avoided being this honest with people for a long time – there are certain relationship truths that you know you can't come back from once they've been shared. I'd kept some things secret partly because I was still hoping they would change, and partly because I knew deep down how bad they really were.

It had been a brutal few months of gathering up enough momentum to close the door on that relationship and keep it closed. It wasn't the first time that things had ended, but this time was different. It had to be different, because I had no part of myself left to give.

I knew that I should have left the first time. Or the second time. Or the third. But I didn't. I stayed after the trust was broken. I stayed after the lying. I stayed through the indecision. I stayed through so much that I told myself I would never tolerate.

I had become the type of woman who stayed in the relationship long after she should have left. And I barely recognised myself.

* * *

I was never the girl who got chased around the playground at break time. In fact, when my more forward friends tracked down their first 'husbands' at age seven and invited us all to the alcove round the corner for the ceremony, I was most often designated as the priest.

It was a trend that had swept through my year group quicker than chicken pox: find someone to marry at break time, and make it official away from the worried eyes of the adults. I could never be as bold as the girls who marched up to their sporty crush and proposed without even making small talk first. I was confident in just about every area of my young life, but telling boys I liked them? No way was I ready for that level of rejection.

We started setting up a couple of ceremonies a day, with one of us on lookout to warn if a teacher was coming round the corner. We treated these marriages with the same attitude that we had towards the bogeyman – we knew they weren't real... but were they? Probably not... but what if they actually were?

In my role of officiator, I asked my peers whether they would be kind, and honest, and faithful (whatever that meant), and whether they took each other to be husband and wife. I got too scared of the teachers finding us to say the part about kissing, but someone else would always say it because let's face it, that's what we were there for.

One girl, let's call her Sarah, took her marriage very seriously. She expected to be saved a seat next to her new husband in every class. She expected him to wait for her at lunchtime. She let him know that rather than running around the field with the boys he had to be available for hand-holding at all times. She wanted notes that she could secretly read in class and, of course, she wanted everyone to know that they were now committed to each other. Which meant there would be categorically no talking to other girls.

They had a blissful honeymoon period of two whole school days until the boy was paired with a girl called Hayley for a science lesson and that was that. It was over. In true primary school fashion, Sarah didn't deliver the break up herself, but sent a messenger with a 'ur dumped' note in their hand.

I don't think I have witnessed such firmly held relationship boundaries since that day. That girl laid out her expectations (as intense as they were), and shut everything down the second they weren't met. Back then we all had the most unwavering ideas about what love should be, long before any of us would actually experience it.

It's easy to make rules about what you will and won't accept in a romantic relationship before you've had a chance to really be in one. We've all had unshakeable opinions about cheating, chores, how a partner needs to speak and act and treat us.

Of course, I wouldn't take them back after that, people don't change.

If he doesn't bring me flowers every weekend, he doesn't deserve me.

If you're meant to be with someone, it's easy.

You deserve to be worshipped and nothing less.

And we really do believe in those standards. In theory, we know exactly what a good relationship is and exactly when it's time to leave and we wouldn't settle for anything in between.

But something seems to happen when we leave theory and enter the practice of an actual relationship. We bend expectations here and there (no big deal). We compromise on a want or a need. We ignore the knowing deep in our stomach that's sensing red flags on repeat. Sometimes we even forgive things we never thought we would. We stay. We lose sight of the standards we had and even the kind of person we were when we set them.

It just isn't as easy to hold onto theoretical rules once we've handed over our hearts and got them all tangled up with another person's. I'd learned that the hard way.

* * *

When my friend's words about being the type of woman who would stay in a bad relationship hit me from across the table, they tap into every bit of shame on the way down.

He was right. I'm not meant to be the kind of woman who forgives the same selfish decisions over and again. I'm not meant to let anyone make me feel small – and especially not a man! Not these days, anyway.

I'm meant to be bold and unapologetic. Unwaveringly feminist in theory and practice. I'm meant to set the bar for how I deserve to be treated and be willing to walk away when someone doesn't meet my standards *the first time around*. I'm meant to be strong. At least, that's how I always imagined I would be when it came to falling in love.

Truthfully, I knew for several months that there was a gnawing distance between what my relationship really was and the standards I should have been holding for myself. But it is all too easy to let those standards slip when there is a promise of happily ever after on the other side.

I started to cling on to the *what ifs* for dear life.

What if he really does want to change?

What if I could learn to be better so that he doesn't do those things anymore?

What if I end it and then it turns out he's The One?

If romanticising the potential of a partner over their reality were an Olympic sport, I'd have won gold.

And I suppose there is something about the type of woman I am that contributed to me staying so long.

I am an empathetic woman – always searching for the reasons behind why people behave in the ways they do and overly sympathising when something traumatic has led to them being the type of person who is careless with others.

I am an understanding woman – always willing to hear someone out and give them a chance to explain their perspective, why they did the thing they did.

I am a hopeful woman, who wants to believe that we all have the capacity to be good, to do better, to love more fully.

I wouldn't want to change being that type of woman, even though I know those traits can easily be taken advantage of when left in the wrong hands.

Still, there was something about that phrase – "the type of woman who would stay", that I couldn't seem to swallow...

In my life I am fortunate enough to be surrounded by badass, powerhouse women. Absolute forces who take no shit and know exactly who they are. Women who've built successful businesses, raised entire families, fought to build better lives for themselves and people around them. Women with the strongest of values who, theoretically, would never stay anywhere their worth wasn't recognised.

And over the years I have watched even the strongest of them break off parts of themselves for the promise of being loved. Forgive things they never thought they would. Accept less than the standard they'd set. Fall for the potential over the reality because *what if...*

We have spent lifetimes being taught that the most important thing we can be is chosen. That the fairytale doesn't start until *they* come along. That romantic love will make everything complete.

We grow up on the promise of happily ever after while simultaneously having our self-esteem systematically undermined by a culture that tells us in every way that we are not enough: not thin enough, not pretty enough, not smart enough, not polite enough, not likeable enough. When you combine those things together, *of course* we stay in bad relationships for longer than we should. Because there is a part of us, small and not sure we're really worthy of love at all, that is just so fucking thankful to be chosen.

And I'm not sure if there is a *type* of woman who is entirely resistant to that. Even the strongest women can want to be loved so much that it becomes a weakness. Even the most intelligent women are sometimes tricked. Even the most emotionally stable women can be unsteadied. Even the most empowered women are sometimes convinced to make disempowering choices.

A lot of us have the potential to be *the type of woman who would stay*, but to suggest that we are at fault for being that is an oversimplification, and a misplacement of blame that once again lands on the ones who have endured the most hurt. Instead of making an archetype of the type of woman who would stay, surely we should be focusing on the type of men who cause women so much pain and still convince them to stay...

But I didn't say any of that in response to my friend's comment. I said that I didn't think I would have stayed either, and moved the conversation along.

* * *

Growing up, the most common kind of date to be asked on was a group date. This basically meant that a bunch of you were hanging out as friends, and there just happened to be a romantic subtext between two of the people there.

When I was twelve, obsessed with My Chemical Romance and metal studded belts, I spent my Saturdays loitering at a local park with a handful of kids who all wore a lot of black but couldn't agree on exactly how to identify (Grungers? Emos? Scene kids? Goths?).

We slumped around drinking energy drinks and watching the one guy who knew how to use his skateboard. Occasionally someone would have a cigarette or start a hushed conversation about Ouija boards.

I was always surprised to have been accepted into the group. Sure, I had my chequerboard sweatbands and dyed blue-black hair that covered half of my face, but I cared way too much about everything to really be part of a gang who appeared to care so little.

I worried that we were taking up too much space in the park and swearing too loudly when there were families around. If I had homework to finish over the weekend then I would be a no-show, giving a much more rebellious reason for my absence the week after. I tried very hard to make engaging conversation which apparently wasn't the point (we were supposed to just linger around, looking the part).

But despite not feeling like I fitted into the group, I kept coming back because, of course, there was a boy.

A boy shaped like a runner bean with skin pale enough to pass for a Romantic poet and dark hair that he flicked away from his eyes, plus skinny jeans that looked like they'd been spray painted on. His name was Eddy, and he was the perfect target for a pre-teen crush.

As the weeks passed, I started to edge slightly closer to wherever he sat in the group, my body buzzing with the brazen energy of closing the gap between us. I moved from the bench to the grass. From the grass to the wall. From the furthest brick, gradually closer until only one other person separated my legs from his. One day I offered him a sip of my giant bottle of knock-off Red Bull and he accepted, putting his mouth where he knew mine had been seconds earlier. He didn't even wipe around the edge of it first.

With some gentle digging, I got hold of his email address, which meant that I could add him on MSN, the online chat site I spent most of my adolescence logged into. We sent a few 'wuu2?'s and 'lol's and 'brb's (I was never totally convinced that he knew who he was talking to).

One day, I made the desperate decision to tell another girl in the group that I had a crush. She'd always made it her business to transport gossip from one person to another, so it was almost guaranteed that it would get back to him.

That evening, I logged onto my online chat, and waited. A painful few minutes passed before his username dinged up on the screen.

Eddydrumboi: Hey
stripey.little.punky.socks: Hiiiii :]
Eddydrumboi: u going cinema on Sat?

stripey.little.punky.socks: Yeah Lol Some Film About A Chicken?
Eddydrumboi: I was thinking...
(Pause for dramatic effect.)
Eddydrumboi: do u wanna go together?
(At this point I jumped up from my chair and span around the room a few times before starting separate chats with three other friends to tell them in real-time what was happening.)
stripey.little.punky.socks: Yeah Sounds Good :] 😄

On the day of my *totally casual not-date* I made my eyeliner extra smudgy and decided to only pad my bra with a tiny bit of tissue paper, so that I wouldn't have to keep worrying about whether it was still boob-shaped while I was moving around.

I got to the cinema and saw my group darkening the corner where you picked up your tickets. Eddy was by the wall with the other boys and I boldly went straight over to where he was leaning. He did not acknowledge my presence.

I tried to chime in with the conversation about some band, but I didn't know them well enough to debate whether or not the drummer was better than the guy from *The Red Hot Chili Peppers*. He still didn't even look in my direction.

I started to wonder what I was doing wrong and whether I should just leave – the boys were visibly uncomfortable at the unspoken tension between me and their floppy-haired friend. When it was time to take our seats, he tried to hang back and offer one of them the space next to me, to which (thank god) the other boy responded that Eddy should really sit next to me, since we were on a date.

On the train that morning, I'd fantasised about sparks zapping between our barely brushing fingers and the prospect of a first proper kiss in the dark of the cinema whilst an animated chicken screamed on-screen about the sky falling. Instead I sat, oscillating between humiliation and rage, hating everything about stupid bird films and stupid boys and stupid tissue clumped up in my top.

After the longest run-time of any film ever, I barged past Eddy and our friends to get out and rushed straight to the fluorescent lights of the bathroom. Nobody came after me, so I composed myself alone and walked out alone to find the group hovering around in the hallway, once again split into the girls and the boys.

As I went to stand with the girls, where I should have been all along, I overheard the same boy who'd encouraged Eddy to sit next to me ask him what he was doing, why wasn't he even talking to me? With his back turned to where I stood, Eddy replied that he didn't really like me, he was still into Hannah, a girl with bouncy blonde hair who'd broken his heart a few months prior. We all heard.

Something about the casual tone of his public rejection summoned the grown woman energy inside of me and I decided that this wasn't it. This wasn't how my first date would end. I would not allow this greasy mop of a boy to humiliate me without consequence!

I turned to him, jabbed his plaid-clad shoulder and asked in my most accusing tone, why he'd bothered to ask me out if he didn't even like me? He mumbled something vague and unconvincing and locked his eyes onto the floor. Everyone was quiet.

High on my own boldness, I went back to the girls and led them out of the cinema, each one telling me how great I'd just been. I decided then and there that he didn't exist anymore. Our chat history would be deleted. His presence at the park on Saturdays would be ignored. His name would be scrubbed from my memory.

Any romantic affection I held towards him was snatched away in a moment. I was left wondering what I'd been so obsessed with? How had I turned an unwashed, inarticulate boy into the man of my fantasies? I'd gotten it so, so wrong. And just like that, the switch flicked back to indifference.

If someone had the audacity to play with my emotions, run hot then cold and not even feel bad about it, they sure as hell weren't getting any more of my attention. That was a standard my twelve-year-old self held firm to.

But the next decade navigating womanhood took its toll on that plucky, confident girl. Diet culture convinced me that I was undesirable. Having big emotions convinced me that I was hard to love. Anxiety about even the smallest life decisions crept in and there I was at twenty-four with a much more malleable set of standards.

* * *

Sometime around 2017, you couldn't log onto social media without a feminist influencer telling you to break up with your boyfriend.

There was a surge of empowered, newly single women shouting about freeing themselves from the patriarchal control of relationships and choosing to love themselves, first. Some of the women were also openly exploring their newly discovered queerness, something that I was slowly considering to be a possibility for myself, too.

I thought that the conversation around reclaiming our energy from unequal relationships with men was brilliant and *so* important for younger generations of women to see. I double-tapped and cheered along, then I made my boyfriend lunch, picked up his dirty socks, sent him money for the train and asked for nothing in return.

I'd grown up alongside the narrative that loving somebody else meant caring for them – physically and emotionally tending to their needs at all times. At least, that's how women were supposed to love.

Women were supposed to nurture, to give endlessly of themselves. Women did the organising and the orchestrating. The preparation and the clean-up. Women made themselves available for the needs of everyone else and learned how to anticipate those needs before they were spoken. Women could carry the weight of whatever was on your plate, and a really good woman would make it her responsibility to help you heal, as well.

When I started over-giving in my relationships, it was with the belief that I would get something back, in the end. At some point, it would be my turn. I would have my meals cooked sometimes, I wouldn't have to bargain for help with the chores, I would be able to put my feet up while someone else planned the details of our life – it wouldn't all be on my shoulders forever.

Like a lot of women, I romanticised the potential of the relationship more than I recognised the reality. I made excuses for my partner's lack of effort, my brain working double-time to over-empathise with all the reasons why he couldn't give anything back.

I was constantly exhausted and constantly frustrated. I felt like I had no energy for anything or anyone but him. The lack of reciprocity in our relationship came out as passive aggression or panic attacks that circled around the prospect of the rest of my life looking like... this.

I was twenty-five and raising a grown man. Which was not how I'd expected things to go.

In the back of my mind, I had a vision of myself – independent, sexually liberated, no more people-pleasing, no more acting small. The woman I thought I'd turn out to be would never have been caught in a relationship so one-sided. So unequal. So... patriarchal.

But I stayed, waiting for 'one day...' and thinking that at least I was loved. At least I was succeeding at being with someone. And maybe that was just the price to pay – the over-giving, the living in lack, the frustration. This man had seen me in my most vulnerable, anxious, unlovable moments and chosen to stick around, so I should be thankful for that, surely?

There's an overused saying about not being able to love somebody else until you love yourself. I don't believe that to be true. I think a lot of people who are lacking in self-love are experts at loving everybody else. But what I have come to believe over time, is that we accept the love we believe that we deserve.

Believing, deep down, that we aren't worth very much won't stop us from being able to love someone else, but it will set the standard for the kind of love we're willing to accept. If your self-worth is on the floor and someone comes in offering the bare minimum, you'll be grateful to bow down and scoop up any crumbs they drop. You won't believe you deserve more than that.

We teach people how to love us. We teach them what we will and won't accept, what we expect in return for what we put in. So, when we fall into relationships without setting any standards, just trying to be perfect or chill or secure the other person's approval regardless of whether we actually like them in return, of course we end up accepting less than we deserve.

Of course, we end up over-giving and taking on roles that never should have been ours. With nothing to disrupt the patriarchal narrative of Good Womanhood and not enough self-worth to demand better, of course, we end up raising grown men, giving away every ounce of our energy, our labour, ending up depleted and tired and even more self-loathing than before.

If we want to change how that story goes, we need two things: first, to truly know our worth. To know that our time and energy and *love* have infinite value, and should be received as such. We need to be able to set a standard for how we deserve to be spoken to, treated and held in our relationships. Which takes knowing our own needs, the kind of love that really fulfils us, and being able to communicate that.

Secondly, we need to be willing to leave. The standards that we set can't simply be optional and left unmet again and again with no repercussions. We can't keep just accepting what we get and telling ourselves we don't really *need* the rest. We don't have to be absolutely ruthless; there can be chances and time for learning and compromise. But we can't lie to ourselves when it becomes clear that we're never going to get the love back that we truly deserve.

We have to be willing to be alone, to move through heartbreak, to take the lessons from that relationship and use them to become new versions of ourselves. It will feel unbearable at times. But it will be a sharp, temporary pain, versus the slow numbing of knowing that you stayed when you shouldn't have.

Over the years, I started building up my self-worth outside of that unequal relationship. I found a brilliant, feminist therapist who encouraged me to tap into all of my human emotions. I started writing more and built a career for myself. I went places and met people and thought a lot about the type of woman I wanted to be in the world. And she wasn't the type of woman who stayed when she wasn't getting back the respect, care and effort that she put in.

She was the type of woman who knew when she was being taken for granted, and said no. She was the type of woman who would rather be alone than with some-one, feeling lonely. She was the type of woman who valued her own energy and wasn't going to settle for a version of love without any reciprocity.

She was the type of woman who learned her lesson, and left.

* * *

It was a stubborn autumn evening, and the three of us were on our way to a local pub garden. Do it on neutral ground, had been the advice. Somewhere nobody's emotionally attached to or feels trapped by.

We'd rehearsed who was going to say what, but we all knew that in the moment it depended on which version of our friend we were going to be met with. In the previous months (even just in recent weeks) we'd seen a variety: from drunken lovestruck to barely able to speak through the sobs. We'd done all the things friends were supposed to do: listened, celebrated, held, given advice, offered support, tried to understand, been angry, been forgiving, been protective. This was our first intervention, and our last resort.

Our friend had met the love of her life about a year beforehand. She'd told us about being swept away to restaurants she couldn't afford, to weekend trips abroad with the most mind-blowing sex you could possibly imagine. They talked about emotions for hours. She was bought presents and told that she was the most beautiful woman on Earth. It was like a fairytale on crack.

And in fairness, we all bought into it. We fawned over the pictures of them together and debated what colour our bridesmaid's dresses should be. We couldn't wait to meet the man who had made our friend feel everything she ever wanted to feel!

But by the time we got the opportunity to meet him, he was busy drinking with strangers at the bar and she was in the bathroom distraught because he said that she'd embarrassed him all evening.

Our friend started to arrive with either a storm cloud or a rainbow above her head whenever we saw her – it was never anything in between. Either everything was perfect and she was so in love that she could barely wait to get back to him, or everything was the worst it could possibly be and how could she live without him?

When we tried to suggest that the intensity of the relationship might not be the healthiest of dynamics, her eyes took on a glazed quality and the next sentence she said always started with "I know, but..." We watched her life get smaller as every drama got bigger, and eventually, we decided that it was time to stop being so soft and tell her what we could see clearly from the outside: that this was the kind of volatile, up-and-down relationship that people warn you to stay away from. And that she was losing herself in it.

Personally, I'd been struggling to empathise since the third loop round the rollercoaster. I couldn't understand why you would tolerate someone who made your days feel so unstable. What kind of love makes you feel like you're being worshipped one minute and shipwrecked the next? Surely, no amount of chemistry or excitement was worth never feeling emotionally safe with your person...

Our friend appeared through the garden doors of the pub, wearing a leather jacket and a few days lack of sleep. We were gentle, but firm. We brought up recent examples of things that weren't acceptable. We told her that we love her, and missed her, and that she needed to leave.

It was another few years before she finally did.

She tried to explain it to me afterwards, why she kept going back for so long. She told me that once you've adapted to everything being so heightened, your body starts to expect it. When things are calm, and your partner is contently lying in bed on a Sunday morning with a coffee and no plans to tip the day upside down, something feels... Off. You get so used to your heart being thrown from side to side that when things are still it seems like something's missing. Like it can't possibly be love.

We've been taught in plenty of ways that intensity is the marker of true love.

We've watched the pining boy climb outside the girl's bedroom window or dangle himself off a ferris wheel until she agrees to a date. We've seen the two people who passionately hate each other inevitably collapse into uncontrollable lust and devour one another. We've heard stories about someone who met their partner one week and flew across the world to marry them the next. We've listened over and over again to songs about love that is addictive, all-consuming, can't-breathe-without-the-other-person intense.

And sure, there should be passion and excitement when you're falling in love. But the kind of intensity that knocks you out of reality and feels like the highest of highs is something different. Something that anyone who's felt it knows: also comes with the lowest of lows.

Some years later, it was my turn to learn.

* * *

When I met him, I was the happiest I'd ever been.

It was an intoxicatingly hot summer and my heart was just about feeling whole again. I'd been healing her for the past six months – collecting up the pieces, feeling all there was to feel, readjusting to being single again.

I had hauled myself past the heaviest of the heartbreak, and I was leaning enthusiastically into the idea that it was *my* time. No more prioritising someone else's needs above my own. No more swallowing down emotions and going without. It had been too long since I'd looked out into the world and asked myself what I actually might want. And right then, I wanted to feel something new.

I wanted to remember what it was like to sit across a table from someone and feel fizzy with the possibility of who they might be. I wanted to kiss new people! I wanted little phone buzzes that distracted me during the day and kept me up too late at night. I wanted fun, I was ready to go find it.

First things first: I downloaded a dating app. I spent three hours making my profile with my palms sweating and my best friend at the other end of the sofa, for support. The prospect of being able to connect with thousands of cute people from the comfort of my phone felt so exciting that I'm pretty sure I did nothing else for at least seventy-two hours.

The anti-climax of online dating came swift and righteous, but I kept up enough momentum to get a couple of dates under my belt. They weren't disastrous or mind-blowing – they were just what I needed.

I started moving through the world with the energy that comes when you're single and ready for adventure. I started saying yes to more things and going to new places. I fell deeper in love with my friends and spent time getting to know myself. My style evolved, my priorities changed, I didn't want to waste another second feeling stuck or lonely or small.

Finally, I was becoming the version of me I always thought I would be. But it was early days in the evolution, and for every carefree week running around the city there were still bouts of grief. There's no such thing as flicking a switch and being healed from heartbreak – it's always a dance between who you were and who you're trying to become. Which is the perfect moment for someone to step underneath your feet, and change your trajectory.

When he first walked into the room, everybody looked up. Partly because he was late, and partly because you couldn't not. He was well dressed, radiating arrogance, and none of us had seen him before. *He could be fun*, I thought.

For two weeks, we spun through a daze of last trains home and dopamine overload. I'd never felt chemicals like it.

Every day came with showers of compliments and promises. He texted constantly, sent videos before going out, and woke me up with phone calls from outside the club saying how much he wished I was there. I'd never felt so wanted. It was like I'd been dying of thirst for years and suddenly I was riding a tidal wave.

He told me that he planned to make me his girlfriend and I knew that I would let go of my own plans. Whatever this was, I had to keep feeling it.

The first big crash came just a handful of weeks later when I found out he'd broken my trust. That's when I should've jumped ship. But I didn't. He wove together an apology and more promises of how much better he could be, how I was more than enough and, of course, it wouldn't happen again!

Of course, it did happen again. And again. And I stayed because after every shattering low, were the kind of highs I'd never felt before.

When we were good, we were euphoric. Absolutely drunk on each other. Nothing else existed. I lost entire weeks with him – couldn't focus on anything else, not work, not friends, not taking care of myself. I realise now that the highs felt so high precisely because they were sandwiched between excruciating lows – they felt rare and intoxicating, like I had to get all I could before they went away again.

The waves were continuous. And as the months added up, I told myself that at least I was getting better at surviving them.

My body woke up to the reality of the relationship long before my heart did.

In the end, I had nothing left. It took months to see the pattern, and even longer to accept that there was only one way to break it.

One day I was telling a friend how badly I wanted the relationship to work. I said that there was nothing else I could do, I'd tried so hard – it all depended on him actually wanting to change. I was powerless, I said. My friend replied, gently but firmly, that I wasn't powerless; I could leave.

Their words struck me like a challenge to my old self – the one who knew exactly how powerful she was – to come back and finally close the door.

So, I took my power back the only way I could. I packed up my lessons, put my heart back in my chest, and drove forwards through the next heartbreak.

* * *

If you've ever asked for advice on whether to end a relationship, you know how many people there are ready to tell you exactly when it's time to leave.

There are three-strikes-and-you're-out people.

There are end-it-at-the-first-sign people.

There are people with a zero-tolerance cheating policy.

There are people who stay through all kinds of fuckery because they've clung onto the idiom that relationships aren't meant to be easy.

The inconvenient truth is that not a single person in this world can tell you when it is time to leave. Not a single other person knows how it feels to exist within your own heart like you do. You are the *only* one who really knows. You are the only one who can call it.

I can't tell you when it's time to leave, and I don't need to. Because you know. You know when you no longer feel like yourself in a relationship. You know when there's the kind of hurt you can't come back from. You know when the thought of spending your life with them feels like it just doesn't fit. And you know when the thing that's stopping you from leaving is fear.

I can't tell you when it's time to leave, but I can tell you that you will survive it.

It will hurt like a motherfucker, and you will endure it. It will be lonely, and you will get better at being alone. It will change you, and one day you will be so glad that it did.

You will never be the only one going through it – there will be songs and books and films to keep you company. You will reconnect with your platonic loves and find support in places you didn't know it could be.

You'll cry. A lot. You'll find different ways to process the pain: making art, moving your body, going somewhere new.

You will collect back all the pieces of yourself you gave away when you were with them, and slowly, you'll grow into a new version of yourself.

You will question whether you made the right choice and time will answer.

One day you will look back and realise that it couldn't have been any other way. It all happened as it was supposed to. And here you are: bigger than you've ever been before.

THE DATING GAMES

I used to be an expert shapeshifter when it came to dating. Not only would I turn into a different person in a relationship, I would be exactly the person whoever I was dating was looking for.

You're attracted to women who are sexually confident and unapologetic? I can be that! You want someone to spontaneously travel with over a long weekend? Let me pack away my anxiety and grab my passport! You need a woman who laughs at your awful jokes and bats her eyelashes even when you say something borderline offensive? I'm your girl! Pick me!

A lot of women are brilliant at morphing into what they think the other person wants because we've been taught that the point of dating is to secure the desire of the other person, *not* to show up as our whole selves with openness and curiosity and explore the possibility of a genuine connection. Even Taylor Swift sings the lyric "Find out what you want, be that girl for a month."

We treat dates more like auditions than the low-pressure experiments they should be. Are we impressive enough *to them?* Are we attractive enough *to them?* Are we what *they* want? We become so absorbed in the worry of whether they like us that whether we like *them* becomes an afterthought. We pack away our real personalities and idiosyncrasies and prepare to perform whatever our potential partner desires. What a disservice to everyone involved!

You don't get to be you. They don't get the chance to know you. Everyone loses.

Sure, you might come away with the short-term validation of being wanted, but you send yourself the message that you're not worthy of being seen, and ultimately, not worthy of being loved, as exactly the person you are.

The performance I most often put on was of the perfect 'Cool Girl' archetype – low expectations, no boundaries, no stress. The Cool Girl doesn't care if you show up late, if you say something rude, or if another girl texts you on the date. She doesn't care about commitment or romance and she doesn't get offended easily. The Cool Girl doesn't have anxiety or need plans – she goes with the flow and wants for nothing extra. She is the epitome of what men are describing in their dating profiles when they say they want a girl who "doesn't take herself too seriously".

The Cool Girl is a patriarchal wet dream, embedded in our consciousness as the most attractive way to be, backed up by every narrative about how *unattractive* it is when women are *too emotional, too needy, too clingy, too desperate.* Although let's remember: a woman will always be too emotional to a man who is emotionally inept.

And, of course, the Cool Girl is definitively, completely, absolutely *not like other girls.*

Other girls with their expectations and their complaints. Other girls with their rom-com fantasies and pumpkin spice lattes. Other girls with their stereotypical femininity and justified reactions to bad behaviour that gets rebranded as craziness.

We can't be seen to be like *other girls* if we want to be the one who's chosen. We have to stand out while simultaneously condemning the rest of our gender so that our partner doesn't have to interrogate their own misogyny and where the negative connotations of 'other girls' actually come from.

When you break it down, the way to make sure that you're *not like other girls* is to have no emotion, no needs and not enjoy anything that's thought to be feminine. It forces us to flatten girlhood into an easily disposable archetype and not dare allow ourselves access to any part of it.

It requires us to not only see ourselves as different from, but *better* than 'other girls'. How much better we are depends on how much distance we can put between ourselves and all things feminine (while still, of course, visually adhering to every feminine beauty standard without complaint).

I used to take a lot of pride in being *not like other girls*, especially when a man told me so. It felt like the ultimate compliment, an affirmation that I'd successfully transcended above the rest of my gender. But ultimately, it was other girls who picked me up from the floor when those men dropped me.

It was other girls who taught me how to stand up for myself. It was other girls who inspired me to find the joy in life and get excited by small things like different flavours of coffee and dressing in bright colours. It was other girls who helped me navigate and unlearn every patriarchal expectation. Other girls are the best thing that's happened to me. Why would I betray them for something as fleeting as being chosen by a man?

Girls who strive to be *not like other girls* in order to win male attention – also known as pick-me girls – have gotten a lot of criticism in recent years, and while there's no denying how harmful it is to leave that kind of internalised misogyny unchecked, pick-me behaviour is a direct result of patriarchal disdain for femininity, coupled with patriarchal conditioning on women to measure their worth by how well they can secure male validation. In other words, we didn't make this shit up ourselves.

Those of us who've fallen into the trap of saying that we're *not like other girls*, might simply be trying to explain that we are complex. We can't be reduced to a stereotype. We are different from the model of girlhood that's been laid out in front of us. But the truth is that *every* girl is more complex than that stereotype. And by distancing ourselves from *other girls*, we are only reinforcing the idea that the stereotype is real.

I no longer take pride in thinking that I'm not like other girls. I take pride in knowing that I am the best parts of all the girls I know and I wouldn't be here without them. I will not betray other girls in order to be thought of as superior. And if that means I miss out on being chosen, I'd consider that a victory; why would I want to be with anyone who has so much unexamined contempt for my entire gender?

There are so many ways that we mould and shrink ourselves to become what we think the person we're dating wants. But one thing ties all the ways together: we can't keep them up forever. At some point the real us will come bounding through the door, demanding to be seen and heard, and that isn't a bad thing! That's where the possibility of a real relationship starts – between people who are flawed and complex and made up of everything that's ever happened to them plus more.

What if we chose to skip the performance at the start and get straight to the good bit? No more malleable personalities and people-pleasing, just showing up whole and being okay with the possibility that it won't be a good match?

What if we focused more on how we *felt* in the other person's company than whether or not they wanted us?

What if we were our full selves?

One thing we need before we can do that though, is to know who the hell we are.

* * *

When I started dating after my long-term relationship, it dawned on me as soon as I downloaded the first app that I didn't have a clue how to describe myself. What music did I like? We'd always just listened to whatever he put on. What were my hobbies, besides things I organised for us to do together? How do you state your dating communication style when you've been having the same conversations with the same person for years? All those little boxes glared at me, waiting.

I suddenly felt so uninteresting. So inexperienced. Swiping through all these people with their niche interests and big adventures and there I was, having primarily identified as someone's girlfriend for the first part of my adult life. Who was I, outside of that relationship?

I realised that if I was going to start dating, then I also had to date myself. I had to grant myself the time and space to figure out what I really liked – what did *I* want to listen to? What did *I* want to eat? How did *I* want to spend my Saturdays? How did *I* like to be touched?

The time I spent alone didn't have to feel like I was just waiting to be chosen by the next person. I could choose myself in that time! I could make lists of things I want to do and *do* them! I could dress in ways that make me feel unmistakably *me* when I pass by my reflection. I could reclaim things I used to love but gave up because they didn't fit conveniently in the schedule before. I could get to know myself so well that when the next person came along there's no way I would be able to be anyone but me.

I decided that I wanted to be the type of person who reads poetry while they have their morning coffee. I ordered some books and carved out my first hour. The more poetry I read, the more I felt inspired to write, and the more healed my heart felt.

I remembered that I actually fucking love music. I grew up belting pop girl anthems in my bedroom, I wore out my first copy of Avril Lavigne's debut album, my inner emo kid still wanted to hear Fall Out Boy and my grown self wanted to dance to Motown in the kitchen on a Sunday morning.

I'd been unbothered about music for so many years – partly because he never asked what I wanted to listen to, and partly because I was scared of the emotions that I would find waiting for me there. I went back to the artists I loved before. I made playlists of all the new songs I found that made me feel something. I blasted anthems to heartbreak and love and being alive out of my car window and sang along while I drove without someone else in the front seat.

I reminded myself that my body was mine long before he came along. I bought new toys and new underwear. I took pictures that I never showed anybody. I granted myself permission to explore the fantasies I'd suppressed and got to know myself for hours.

It wasn't all finding out new things about myself – I also worked on accepting the parts that might not look so shiny on my future dating profile...

I am not the spontaneous adventure girl who hops on planes with no details planned – I would like every single detail clearly laid out at least a week before the event, thank you. I have no interest in hanging out in expensive bars with people who don't really talk about anything – I'd much rather be by myself, playing *The Sims*. I *do* happen to take myself quite seriously – not necessarily by choice, but that's the brain I'm working with.

And I knew that if I was ever going to connect with someone, genuinely, then I couldn't hide those things. I couldn't wish them away and go back to being an amorphous woman ready to mould to what the next man wants. I would show up as me. And I wouldn't abandon myself at the threat of being disliked. I couldn't – I knew myself too well.

* * *

This could actually be something... I thought to myself while walking back to the tube on a chilly Thursday evening.

We were on date number three, and we'd spent the last half of it shamelessly kissing in public and feeling smug about what we might have found. Our humour seemed to match. Our conversation wove seamlessly between light-hearted anecdotes and deeper meaning-of-life stuff. We were *definitely* attracted to each other. It was all coming up roses.

I allowed myself to float in the feeling of possibility on the way home. They'd already texted with an inside joke and I smiled giddily at my phone.

We went on messaging until the early hours – a quickly adopted routine since we'd met a couple of weeks earlier. I went to sleep feeling like my lungs were filled with little sparkles and looked forward to speaking to them the next day.

When the light crept through my curtains, I rolled awake and reached for my phone and the dopamine boost that would propel me out of bed. There was no good morning message. *Strange* I thought, and wondered how to craft my own excited wake-up text to kick start another day of back and forth.

Morning! Hope you slept well :) I'm still thinking about those burgers we had yesterday, SO good and the company made the night even more delicious :) x

The anticipation of the reply tickled my insides as I made coffee, showered and wrote my daily to-do list.

I was skating on the high of the night before and filling every spare moment with thoughts of potential futures.

Maybe we'd go on holiday together, lounge effortlessly around a pool and devour each other at night. Maybe they'd be the next person I introduced to my family – charming everybody and making each tradition richer. Maybe we'd move in together, get a dog and a big velvet sofa and have friends over for sun-soaked afternoons on the patio outside... Maybe.

By lunchtime, I still hadn't heard back. A sourness started to tinge the edges of my high. As the rest of the day passed with radio silence, my drunken euphoria curdled into a hangover, complete with anxious over-thinking and nausea.

Did I do something they didn't like? Did I say the wrong thing? What if something's happened to them? What if this was all in my head? I went to bed with a pit of dread in my belly. I decided to send one more message.

Are you ok? I'm headed to bed now, sweet dreams and hopefully talk tomorrow x

Two days later, I got a lacklustre message about being busy and some other platitudes that didn't invite a response. I replied, gently questioning whether things between us were okay and reassuring them that they could be honest. I didn't hear back. Something had changed. I didn't know what and I never would. All I knew is that one day I was floating, and the next I'd come crashing back down to a reality I didn't understand but had to accept: they weren't interested.

My natural response – especially since I didn't get the real reason – was to excavate every part of myself in search of the hideous flaws that had turned them off. Surely it was the way I ate... Or maybe I over-shared about my childhood... It could have been what I wore... They probably noticed the breakout on my cheek that I'd tried to hide with make-up... They were obviously disgusted by me... I must be an awful kisser... Oh god, nobody else is gonna want to date me...

When we're left without an explanation, our brains go into overdrive to find one. We *must* make sense of the situation, however we can. And the best way a lot of us have learned to do that, is to turn inward and find parts of ourselves to blame. If we can establish that the problem is with us, we can at least feel a sense of control, and if we punish ourselves enough, maybe we can stop it happening again.

The spiral from pinpointing our imperfections to deciding that we're unlovable happens so fast we barely notice it. And just like that, we pick up a new dent in our self-esteem that we carry onto the next part of our lives.

It feels impossible to hold onto logic when the soft parts of ourselves have been hurt. If I was being logical, I might have considered any number of explanations for why they were no longer interested that didn't have much to do with me at all.

Maybe they realised that they weren't ready to be in a relationship. Or perhaps an ex popped up and complicated things. Maybe our conversations had triggered something in them that they didn't want to deal with. Or maybe, just maybe, they actually *didn't* like me.

It was possible that I wasn't their type. Or that they'd thought we weren't compatible. Maybe I *did* say or do something they didn't like. But that doesn't automatically mean that I did something *wrong*, it just means I showed them part of myself that was wrong *for them.* And if they think that I'm wrong for them, then, *of course* they're not right for me.

My best friend cooked us dinner while we unpacked every detail of the short-lived affair. We agreed that rather than romanticising the idea of them based on the performance they gave when things were good, I had to accept that their actions were also a clear indicator of who they were. And instead of obsessing over what they might not like about me, I had the right to ask myself whether I still liked them.

Did I want to be with someone who thinks that slow ghosting is an acceptable way to communicate?

Am I attracted to people who don't have the strength and confidence to weather difficult conversations?

Do I want someone who doesn't one hundred percent want me?

The answer was a resounding no.

I set about the business of taking them down from the pedestal I'd built them in my mind. I amped up my self-care and reminded myself of how lovable, desirable and worthy I was – to myself first and foremost. And I put our brief encounter in its place, amongst the collection of interactions and relationships that weren't meant to be anything more than what they were.

Rejection sucks. Whether it comes swiftly off the back of the first interaction or whether it trickles in slowly after you've already started to invest in the possibility of them. It will always hurt, and it will always be far too easy to blame ourselves and decide that we are unlovable.

We are allowed to be hurt – we're allowed to wallow and wish that things had been different. But we cannot afford to abandon ourselves just because someone else doesn't see our worth. We *know* that sometimes things not working out have nothing to do with us, and everything to do with them. And ultimately, if they don't want us, we're smart enough to know they're not the one.

The one wouldn't ghost. The one wouldn't be hot and cold. The one wouldn't let us go.

Their rejection does not need to become our new narrative. They're the one who will never get a chance to know us, explore us, enjoy us, love us the way that we do. Sucks for them.

* * *

I have sat through far too many bad dates.

I have sat through dates with people who talk endlessly about themselves without asking me a single question. I have sat through dates with people who've laughed at my job and haven't been able to tell the difference between my eyes and my boobs. I have sat through dates with people who thought *The Human Centipede* was an appropriate film for a romantic evening together.

Even during dates when I would rather implode than listen to another second of a man explaining the crypto

marketplace over over-priced cocktails in a too-loud restaurant, I have stayed, because leaving early has always
been unthinkable.

Leaving a date early is the boss level of romantic
boundary setting; the ultimate example of protecting
your time and energy over doing what's expected of
you. Letting someone know that you're not feeling a connection and cutting your time together short takes the
kind of self-assured confidence that I could hardly have
imagined growing up.

In my teenage years, when I was newly developed and
navigating men's sudden interest in my body, I had no
clue how to turn them down when I wasn't interested
in their attention. I would freeze, deer-in-headlights, too
scared to potentially detonate their ego with a 'no', too
often ending up giving them a phone number I didn't
want them to have, or agreeing to a date I didn't want
to go on.

Rejecting someone romantically is uncomfortable for
most people, but there are extra layers of discomfort
for women when it comes to shutting down romantic
advances from men. And beyond discomfort, there's fear.

Most boys are not raised to accept and respect a girl's
'no'. The entitlement that a lot of men feel over women
and their bodies begins in boyhood, growing up in a culture of normalised objectification of women, where they
learn to see girls as things to use for their own desires,
rather than as whole human beings whose voices should
be listened to.

Too many depictions of romantic and sexual relationships perpetuate the idea that a woman's 'no' simply

means 'try harder'. Time and time again we've seen the male character persist in his pursuit of an uninterested woman to the point of harassment, ignoring her 'no' until he gets what he wants. And we're meant to believe that this is romance.

Toxic masculinity prevents boys from learning how to healthily process their emotions, and green-lights aggression as an acceptable masculine response – especially to anything that threatens the ego. We have witnessed, too often, how violent men can become when they're rejected by women.

So if you're a woman who dates men, there is the inescapable question of whether it's safe to say 'no', to reject the proposition or leave the date early. After all, "Men are scared that women will laugh at them, women are scared that men will kill them."

Beyond the fear for our physical safety, there is the fear of overstepping the parameters of polite womanhood, and being labelled as 'rude', 'selfish', 'intimidating' or 'crazy'. These words have all been successfully weaponised to force confident, assertive and strong-willed women back into their assigned place within patriarchy.

We're taught that being 'nice' is always the priority, despite how much of a shitty time we might be having. Being agreeable is more important than listening to our intuition. Being polite is more important than our time. Especially during interactions with men, our role is meant to be that of the deferential listener, smiling sweetly as they mansplain the basics of a subject we happen to have a degree in. Even if we're uncomfortable, uninterested or offended, being honest, inserting our opinion or ending the conversation risks us being branded with the gendered insults we've spent lifetimes trying to avoid.

I learned early that one of the worst things I could be called was 'rude'. But rudeness is a rigged concept for girls; ensuring we are never perceived as rude means never disagreeing, never voicing discomfort, never showing our dissatisfaction, even when it's warranted. Good girls aren't ungrateful. Good girls don't cause scenes. Good girls prioritise other people's feelings and keep the peace.

The burden of politeness has always weighed more heavily on women than on men. During the Victorian era, women who wished to be part of respectable society were inundated with endless rules dictating the kinds of behaviours that were socially acceptable and which weren't. The way they should speak, dress, move, eat, travel and, of course, engage with men, was described in meticulous detail in handbooks that every socially mobile woman would abide by.

Florence Hartley's popular 1860 guide *The Ladies' Book of Etiquette, and Manual of Politeness* warned women to avoid talking about themselves during conversation: "Never introduce your own affairs for the amusement of the company; such discussions cannot be interesting to others", and reminded them that "True politeness is being polite at all times, and under all circumstances." Sounds disturbingly familiar to how a lot of us have grown up believing we should behave on dates...

Whether it's in a social or professional context, women are still punished for being anything other than polite at all times, and the pressure is only amplified for women who aren't white. Black women have to walk a tightrope of misogyny *and* racism when expressing themselves in order to avoid being marked with the angry black woman stereotype, a trope that's existed since the nineteenth century and is used to invalidate *any* reaction outside of quiet deference.

Serena Williams is a prime example of how this kind of misogynoir manifests: perhaps the greatest athlete of all time who has been wrongfully penalised, tone policed and racially mocked in media throughout her entire career, for reactions that go unpunished from her white, male counterparts. The many media pile-ons of Meghan Markle are proof of how deeply a woman's character will be assassinated when she does anything that can be perceived as selfish, even when, in reality, she is only setting boundaries and making decisions that protect her own well-being.

When it comes to advocating for ourselves and shutting down situations we don't want to be in – especially romantic situations – there is a minefield of potential consequences for women to navigate. But even taking all of them into account, I still believe that we *have* to learn how to stand firm and unwavering in our 'no', because until we do, we will never have full ownership over our own lives.

The same burden of politeness and fear of being seen as rude that shows up in our romantic lives impacts every part of our existence.

We sit through situations we don't want to be in, whether it's a date or a film at the cinema, too scared to leave in case we disturb other people's experience and come off as inconsiderate. We're terrified to send our food back in a restaurant, even if it's stone-cold or burnt through, because asserting our preferences would make us a nuisance. We don't speak up when something's wrong at work, in case we're seen as bossy or aggressive.

We sacrifice our time, our needs and our voices in order to please other people and stay within the confines of polite womanhood. And it has to stop. Because the thing that we really sacrifice in the end, is ourselves.

We have to realise that there is a difference between being impolite, and simply advocating for ourselves. For too long, politeness has been used as a social convention to keep us quiet and preserve the patriarchal status quo, which does not deserve to be preserved.

We need to understand that what's often branded as selfishness in a woman is her refusing to continue putting other people's needs above her own, and reclaiming what she's expected to give away.

If we want to become the kinds of women who are capable of leaving bad dates, we need to start teaching ourselves a new narrative. One where mildly inconveniencing the people around us doesn't make us a nuisance – it just makes us a person as worthy of our space as anyone else there. One where asserting our needs doesn't make us bad, it makes us our own best advocate and that is something to be *proud* of. One where we realise that our time and energy is just as valuable as everyone else's, and if we don't protect it, who will?

We need to build our assertiveness like a muscle – one uncomfortable situation at a time, because this one life is mine – and yours – and we get to decide how we spend it.

Start with leaving the event as soon as it stops being fun. Don't believe the voice telling you that people are judging you – the reality is that most won't care and the ones who do need something more interesting to care about.

Challenge yourself to request your order exactly how you like it – ask for extra sauce, or a different side, or another drink once you've finished the first one. Voicing your preferences doesn't make you a burden.

Practise saying when you're not completely happy with something – the result will never be as catastrophic as you think.

The sooner we unlearn the people-pleasing, over-apologising and self-sacrificing of polite womanhood, the better every part of our lives will be. Plus, we'll never have to waste a Friday night on a bad date ever again.

BEING SAVED

I would see him most often when I was sitting in the back seat of my dad's trusty old estate car; big enough to fit a family plus baggage. The seats were soft grey and musty from the many owners before, and mum would always take the middle seat to save any of us the discomfort.

A couple of times a year we'd pile in, ready for a budget-friendly adventure somewhere within driving distance. Maybe a small southern town where dad spent his childhood summers, maybe a visit up north to grand-parents cosied up by the sea. Wherever we were driving to, he was always there: leaping over telephone poles, sprinting alongside the window.

I imagined him tall, with gentle curls and kind eyes. A boy who loved me so much he would do anything: surprise me with a visit at school, climb through my bed-room window, defy physics to keep up with me on the motorway on the way to a family holiday.

I'd invented him around the same time I realised that none of the boys in my year group were quite what I needed them to be. They weren't attentive or emotionally intelligent. Most of them couldn't yet hold a conversation. And perhaps most importantly, none of them liked me.

But the boy of my dreams did.

The most perfect thing about him was that he under-stood me completely. He understood why I sometimes felt sad and misunderstood in the back of the car. He understood why I felt embarrassed or scared at school. He understood why I was crying in my room and he didn't love me any less because of these emotions. I didn't even need to find ways to explain them to him, he just *knew*. And that was real love.

I never saw him as a knight. There were no tall towers or castles or evil curses. But he would save me in his own way – from loneliness, from not being seen, from being left with just me and my big emotions. He would save me from myself.

We've all been sold the fairytale saviour in one way or another. The princess trapped in the tower who can only be freed by the perfect suitor. The girl who spends all day and night sweeping before a prince swoops in and changes everything. The career woman who doesn't understand happiness until she's finally chosen by a man.

The narrative that romantic love will be the thing to save us is inescapable. And don't get me wrong, romantic love can be transformative, powerful, euphoric! But to hold it up as the only thing that will finally make all the other things okay leaves us all desperately searching, and putting our hearts in danger along the way.

* * *

I had my first real relationship with someone I met in a nightclub. While my friends saw going out to bars and clubs as a way to relax and have fun, I saw it almost *exclusively* as a chance to be chosen.

I was eighteen and at the height of my body hatred, so going out always involved a layer of SPANX, bra inserts and panic about the calories in alcohol. I would crash diet in the days leading up to the night out so that my stomach could be as flat as possible before stuffing myself into the smallest shapewear I could find.

Then, after hours of getting ready, outfit adjustments, imagining what I would look like to everybody else, I'd spend the evening sucking in and standing strategically, scoping out whether there were any boys who might validate my efforts and choose me. And maybe that boy would be the one.

The one whose validation would give my brain a break from thinking of nothing but numbers. The one whose want for my body might help heal something. If someone else thought my body was desirable, maybe I could too? Maybe them wanting me would save me from what I needed saving from the most. And one fateful Saturday night, there he was.

I'd seen him around before, always with the same group of guys who liked to get off-their-face drunk and into trouble. On this particular night, he was standing in the middle of the bar, having an argument with a girl who I later found out he'd recently broken up with. None of these things jumped out as glaring red flags because I was eighteen and red flags didn't exist to me yet.

Our eyes connected mid-argument, and later that night he came over. We only said a few words to each other before he had to rush out of the club because his friend had gotten into a fight outside. But when we left shortly after, he was still there. He told me that he had to help his friend get home, but if I gave him my number, he would definitely text.

And he did. He texted every day until we saw each other next. He didn't disappear after we'd slept together, like so many of the other boys had. He was the first one who wanted to see me again after. The first one who actually wanted me to be his girlfriend. The first one who chose me.

I waited for it to feel like that fixed everything. Here it was: the validation that I'd been taught my whole life would make everything alright! But weirdly, I only seemed to become more aware of all the parts of myself I didn't like in the light of being wanted.

I was extra self-conscious of my body, always worrying that he'd spot me at an unflattering angle and be horrified. I flinched every time his hand brushed past my stomach and refused to let him see me without putting make-up on first. Rather than being healing, his want became another pressure that I *had* to keep up with.

My body image issues remained all-consuming. And because I thought so little of myself, I was willing to accept the little he offered me. I was so desperate to be saved from my own self-hatred that I held on, dancing through each red flag and delusionally hoping that he might turn into everything I'd ever wanted.

I really believed that having the external validation of being desired by this man would save me. But it quickly became clear that that just wasn't how it worked. If anybody was going to be able to save me from the way I saw myself, that person was going to have to be me.

And that's exactly what I did.

* * *

You know that famous quote, "Wherever you go, there you are"? To me, it perfectly captures the (sometimes horrifying) reality that you can't outrun yourself.

At some point, everybody fantasises about running away, starting fresh on an island or a commune or a country where people spend afternoons perched on pavements, sipping coffee and watching the world go by. And generally, the crux of the fantasy is that in that world, we are different.

We won't have the same worries or burdens or feel bad about any of the things that keep us up at night in our current reality. We'll be more spontaneous, more creative, more carefree. We'll wear things we've never had the courage to wear before and our hair will fall perfectly into place without any effort or adjustment as the sun sets behind us.

And sure, a change of scenery and a new adventure can work wonders, but ultimately, once the fantasy plays out, you will still be you. The parts of your life and yourself that you're running from will inevitably catch up in one way or another, sprouting through the cracks of the fantasy until they're unignorable.

For a lot of us, the magical place that we believe will change us into a new person is a relationship.

Once we are loved, we won't feel bad about ourselves anymore. We won't get stressed over the small things. We won't be as hurt by our traumas – they'll all melt away and we'll be left fresh and new, awash in being wanted: saved.

But the old phrase still rings true: *'Wherever you go, there you are.'*

We are still ourselves when we enter into relationships. And we still have to *be with ourselves,* even when we're with someone else. No matter how much time we spend attached to another person, we are still the one who we go to bed with every night and wake up with every morning. We are still in a relationship with ourselves, first.

Being with someone else doesn't magically erase all the characteristics we're uncomfortable with or wipe out any memory of having been hurt before. In fact, relationships can be the *most* revealing places when it comes to confronting painful parts of ourselves and what we've been through.

A friend of mine recently fell in love for the first time after years of wanting a relationship more than anything. It was the only thing missing from her life, she said, and it would make everything else better. And it did, for a while. I think she was more surprised than anybody when all her old insecurities, anxieties and imperfect habits came flooding into the relationship after a few months. She was still her – working through all the things she was before. But now she had a partner.

A good relationship doesn't automatically turn you into a completely different person, but a good partner does support you while you heal and grow into the next version of yourself. A good partner isn't an all-powerful antidote to everything bad you've ever felt, but they are someone who wants to be there with you while you weather the bad and get back to the good, together. They are not your saviour, but they are your teammate.

When we see our potential partner as the person who's going to save us, we're setting up a power imbalance before the relationship has even started. The saviour is wise and has all the answers, while we're lost and don't know anything. The saviour is strong and doesn't struggle with any of the same things we do. The saviour is better than us. They are our superior.

And that dynamic can be disempowering as hell. It means we put more trust in them than we do in ourselves (the perfect set-up for a partner looking to manipulate us). It means we're in a constant state of comparison where they just seem to be better at everything. It means we can't see them clearly, in all their human imperfection – they can do no wrong! But the thing is, you need to be able to see your partner clearly to build a real connection with them.

Even if your partner has helped you in more ways than you can describe, to place them so far above you is doing yourself a disservice. You also got yourself here. And you are capable of more than you realise, with or without them.

The last time I put a man on a saviour pedestal, I was a shell of myself. Everything about me felt so small: my confidence, my abilities, my goals, my desires. I spent my days navigating extreme anxiety, too scared to go anywhere or do anything. But there he was: the one who would save me from it all.

I conveniently ignored the fact that he was also the one who had put me there.

* * *

"One more chance," he said. The idea of it felt like honey pouring over the cracks in my nervous system.

One more chance for things to be different, to not repeat the same patterns, to not make the same mistakes.

I'd lost count of how many chances there had already been; this whole dance had become far too familiar. Familiar enough for me to know that if I said yes, if I let him back in, there would be at least a few days where things felt better. Where I could let myself believe that this time really would be different and bask in the endorphins of being with him again.

I never saw myself as someone who would entertain an on-again-off-again relationship, but there was no other way to describe what I'd been in for months.

The instability of the relationship seeped out into every crevice of my life – I had never felt so anxious or out of control. I was expecting bad news to be around every corner. I'd stopped trusting my own decisions. I wasn't sleeping or eating properly and I didn't want to see my friends because they would be able to tell how bad it was. I was broken. But there he was, saying one more chance. And god did I wanna take it.

I knew that he was capable of being good to me – sometimes he was perfect... for short periods of time. And what if he really did want to change? What if this was the turning point? That would solve everything! We could float away blissfully together and I would never have to feel this way again. I would be saved!

But expecting to be saved by the same person who broke you is the emotional equivalent of self-harm. It is setting yourself up to be hurt again.

Not only that, but putting our faith in someone who's repeatedly caused us harm to come back and save us undermines our trust in ourselves and *our* ability to be the one who saves us.

It wasn't until after I accepted that the relationship was never going to change that I was able to put the pieces of myself back together again. By putting him in the position of being a saviour, despite all he'd put me through, I had abandoned myself. And it was time to come home.

I had been convinced that he knew better than me, when in reality I had a lifetime of knowing before he came along. I held up all the things he did so easily, that I still struggled with, as evidence of how far above me he was. I gave him the power to make or break me, because when a saviour comes along you give in, and trust whatever they say.

One of the things about him that I always found impressive was his driving. I learned to drive later than most of my friends because I found the whole idea of it terrifying. When I did start lessons, I would leave a patch of sweat on the seat after every hour and need the rest of the day to calm my nervous system back down. Once I passed, I never drove beyond the small-town roads I was familiar with, and would be on the verge of a panic attack anytime I took a wrong turn and landed somewhere unknown.

He, on the other hand, was a big city driver. Fast and confident and borderline reckless. When we went places, he would always choose to drive, not caring about central London rush hour or where he'd find a place to park.

Sitting in the front seat next to him, I felt strangely safe. Like I didn't have to deal with something that made me so incredibly anxious because he had it taken care of. I told myself that I could never be like him, so unbothered and fearless. I was just a small-town girl who never left her comfort zone and there he was, so experienced in all the ways I wasn't.

After too many months of instability, empty promises and earth-shaking ups and downs, I finally remembered who the fuck I was.

I might not have grown up in a big city, but I had overcome things that most people could only imagine. I might not have been as confident as he was in rooms full of strangers, but I would never build that confidence standing behind him. I might have been scared of what would happen if we broke up, but I had been broken and rebuilt myself more than once before him.

He was no saviour. And who the hell said I needed one anyway?

I ended the relationship, for good this time. I moved out of my small town and came to the big city, by myself. I walked through doors into places I would've been too scared to go alone before: bars and restaurants and networking events. I made friends with strangers and said yes more. I learned to trust myself again and I promised to keep my heart safe. I grew, and healed, until I hardly recognised the small, scared girl I was before. And every now and then I remember, while I'm driving through busy London streets with my windows down and music blasting, that once upon a time I thought I would never be able to do this, without him.

The princess saves herself, again.

* * *

As it turns out, no romantic interest of mine – real or imaginary – has ever had the power to save me. Which makes sense, considering they were all only human. And it turned out to be a good thing, in the end.

My first partner and I had the kind of long-term togetherness that feels like every part of your lives is intertwined, fused by time and routine and comfort. My brain couldn't wrap itself around a version of the future that didn't include coming home and finding him on the sofa, smelling his skin every day, fitting my hand into his.

But by the end, I was so tired, so unhappy, so sure that there had to be more to life than raising this man and feeling alone, even when I wasn't.

So, I began the process of breaking my bones away from his – that's the most accurate metaphor I can find for how it feels to leave your first real love after years together. A growing, dawning ache followed by a shattering snap, and months of hurting, healing, hurting, healing.

Once he had moved out of the house we lived in together, I had a lot of time by myself to revisit the best and worst moments of us. I paced, I cried, I yelled, I wrote sad poems and angry poems, I got new bedsheets and asked my friends to confirm that I'd done the right thing.

After a hazy number of days in the house alone, I ended up on the floor, crying harder than I'd ever cried before – deep, animal wails that came from a place I didn't know existed inside me. One thought kept repeating in my mind, pushing the sadness out of every pore: nobody is coming. Nobody is coming back. Nobody is coming to save you.

With every repetition of it I sobbed harder. It felt like one of my greatest fears, confirmed. I cried until I couldn't breathe and my whole face swelled. Nobody was coming to save me – I could cry here by myself for the rest of eternity and nobody would come.

Once my body had used up all its water, I curled into a ball and lay there, feeling the rough carpet on my sensitive face, remembering how to breathe. Some minutes went by and I realised that my brain had gone quiet – exhausted. Then, something told me to get up.

It wasn't so much a voice as a force from somewhere within. I pulled myself up from the carpet, dragged myself over to the nearest mirror, and looked myself dead in the eyes. I had never seen myself look so small.

Then, without thinking about it, I heard myself speak. "You will be okay," my voice said. Then she repeated it. "You will be okay. You will be okay. You will be okay." I felt myself nodding encouragingly at my reflection. My eyes were locked into place, staring into themselves, but now something in them looked different – more armoured, more knowing.

I kept repeating to myself until I believed it. Then I turned around, left the room, and went through the rest of my day.

I didn't tell anyone what had happened for a while because it felt unexplainable – I hadn't consciously made the effort to get up or the decision to start speaking to myself. It had just happened. Like my body had been taken over, like some future version of me was steering. And I really did believe her: that we would be okay. We didn't need anyone to come back and save us (although we could probably do a better job of allowing the right people to support us so we weren't always crying alone). We would keep going. We would heal. *We would save us.*

Not in the dramatic fairytale way but in the real work of showing up for ourselves and believing that we were worth saving. We'd already saved ourselves from worse, before.

When I think back to my first saviour, the imaginary boy who understood me so completely, I realise that he had everything I needed precisely because he came from within me. His knowing was my knowing. His instinct to comfort me was my own. It was all me – I had simply projected my own ability onto a make-believe partner, rather than recognising that I had everything I needed inside me already.

Even though the idea of being saved by someone else is so sweet, so easy, so satisfying, and even though it feels like a loss to let it go, it makes room for something so much more powerful.

It makes room for you.

GOOD LOVE

She walked through the door and I had the unmistakable feeling that she had been there before. That she had always been there, in every chapter, in every timeline.

I was sure that it was her who I had run through fields with when we were young, collecting fruit to eat and feeling all grown up even though we were only just about old enough to be outside by ourselves.

I was sure that it was her who I was looking for in the sky on the nights I couldn't sleep next to the man who'd broken my heart for the umpteenth time.

It felt like she must have been there in every significant childhood memory because suddenly it just didn't make sense that she wasn't. I recognised her as if I'd known her so many times before. Her hands looked as familiar as my own. Her face didn't feel new.

I fell in love with her almost instantly. From the moment I saw her standing, huddled against my radiator for warmth on an unseasonably cold day. I had planned for the next period of my life to be free from commitment, full of personal healing and absolutely not attached to anyone else's heart. But as soon as she showed up, I knew that what I wanted most in the world was to love her exactly the way she needed to be loved. She felt the same, and we set about exploring how that might look.

We both knew exactly what we didn't want. We shared wounds from past loves and were both adamant about how much better the other deserved. We agreed that if nothing else, we would learn to love each other softly; neither of us needed another experience that called itself love but turned out to be harsh, controlling, confusing, full of hurt.

We actively learned what softness meant to the other person. How does soft love behave? How does it feel? What does it bring? How does it communicate? How does it hold?

We learned that soft love will not always be perfect. Sometimes it will misunderstand, sometimes it won't feel like quite enough. Sometimes it will highlight something in ourselves that's uncomfortable to look at. But those moments can be worked through with openness and care, to get back to the good.

Something we've built from learning how to love each other, that I've never experienced before, is a genuine partnership. In past relationships, I've always felt overloaded with responsibility and unable to ask for help – or rather, unable to trust that help would come (without guilt) when I asked for it.

I would manage a two-person household entirely by myself, doing all the cooking, cleaning, shopping, organising. Coming home to find my partner in the same dent on the sofa, not even bothering to get up and help as I wrestled bags through the door.

I would solve every problem myself. Spending hours working things out alone for the benefit of us both, with little recognition or gratitude for the time or emotional labour it took.

And when the world felt like too much, when my brain spiralled into everything that was wrong or when I was swallowed by something hurtful that they'd done, I would lie next to them, feeling completely alone. It's a pervasive kind of pain, being with someone and still feeling like you're entirely by yourself.

Good love feels like having a teammate. Someone who's willing to carry their weight, and yours on the days it feels too heavy. Someone who's on your side in every battle – no jealousy, no personal insecurity getting in the way of them cheering you on. Someone who wants to help not only for what they'll receive in return but because they want your life to be easier.

Good love feels like letting the mask fall. When we first started dating, she would point out whenever she sensed that I was performing: trying to come across as perfect, hiding my needs, focusing too much on how I looked to her. Things we all do in the early days of relationships (and things you learn to do double if you're a woman who's been dating men).

I struggled to let go of the safety blanket of performance. How could this person really see me, want me, love me if I'm not being my shiniest, most desirable self? But I got sick, and she stayed. I had bad days, she loved me the same. I showed up as I was, she said it was a privilege to be the person who gets to hold that version of me. Slowly, I started to trust that she really meant it.

Good love is safe, it doesn't lie awake at night worrying about where the other person is, what they're doing, who they're with. We'd both felt that before, the trickling sense that somewhere out there, your trust is being betrayed and all you can do is wait for the confirmation in the morning.

I'd tried to minimise the pain of being cheated on in the past – *I'm not jealous! I'm chill! I know monogamy isn't for everyone!* It was never the physical act itself of what he'd done that twisted my insides. It was the idea that he could make a fool of me and our relationship by sharing an intimate secret with someone outside of it. It was the fact that my emotions could so easily be removed from his consciousness for the sake of what? A quick hit of dopamine that comes with the validation of a stranger? Good love doesn't prioritise that over security and trust.

There are partners who are proud to be with you – proud to tell people about you, to cheer for you, to hold you next to them in the world, whether you're physically there or not. Then there are partners who are proud of how much they can get away with whilst being with you – proud of doing wrong, proud of their selfish choices, proud of themselves for getting their way. Needless to say, good love can only happen with the first type of partner.

Good love connects to your inner child and invites them to come out: we can be playful and silly and share the things we love with this person without the fear of being abandoned or belittled. We can get out of our heads and into our bodies and follow where we feel the joy without fear that we will be punished for letting go.

One of my favourite things about her is how often she plays. She skips down pathways and hugs trees. We dance in the kitchen and play ping pong on the floor. We pretend to be dinosaurs and talk about imaginary worlds filled with marshmallows and friendly giraffes before we go to sleep. We sing ridiculous songs to each other and run through fields holding hands. We know that we are best friends first, before anything romantic is layered over the top. I didn't realise how healing that could feel.

Good love is stable, steady. In the early months of our relationship, my nervous system didn't quite know how to adapt to what was happening – or what wasn't happening. We were both so used to being ricocheted around, picked up and dropped, flying between extremes and confusing the crash and high of chemicals for great romance.

But here was a different kind of love: one that showed up when it said it would; one that didn't withhold or flood in to create a reaction; one that was consistent and trustworthy. At points it felt like something must be missing – where were the dramatic waves of unreal promises juxtaposed with scraping ourselves up from the floor? Where were the surreal highs and devastating lows, barrelling in one after the other?

As it turns out, good love stays until the expectation of being destabilised fades away. Good love shows up every day until you believe it when it says that it's staying. Good love soothes and calms, until you can breathe easily again and let go of the fear of what's coming next.

Good love encourages you to look after yourself, first and foremost: tend to your own garden, check in with your own needs, not sacrifice too much of yourself to the other or give what you don't have.

I've always been susceptible to over-giving when I'm in love. I would give of myself until there was nothing left, if it meant I could avoid disappointing the other person. But someone who truly cares for you does not want you to run yourself into the ground to appease them. They want you to be well, even if your self-care is sometimes inconvenient for them.

Good love isn't perfect or always easy – there is room for good love to contain bad days, miscommunication, occasional doubt. But good love chooses to work together through the problem, rather than working against the other person.

Sometimes we slip. One of us will say something unknowingly hurtful, or harsher than it needs to be. Sometimes we press down on each other's wounds without realising, and the resolution is hard to find. But once we've felt through our initial reactions and honoured our own feelings, we try our best to understand the other person's. We try to hold onto softness, even when we are hurt, angry or confused. And we've managed to find our way back every time so far.

Good love allows you to be whole. And lets you know that every part of that whole has always been worthy of love. My younger self was so sure that she was too much. My brain has always felt like a maze that I don't dare let anyone else into in case they get lost as well. I have felt like a burden, a problem, a waste of everyone's time. But good love will illuminate the parts of you that you're scared are unlovable, hold them to the light and help you to see them with the compassion you've always deserved.

Good love is built. It doesn't fall ready-made from the sky and slot into your life without a single effort to adapt.

It will test your ability to self-reflect, to evolve, to hold somebody else's heart without dropping your own. Good love takes work – not the kind of work that breaks you down and leaves you barely recognising yourself, but the kind of work that builds you into a better version of yourself.

I was not expecting her to walk through my door and for my heart to say 'we're home', but that's how it went. And wherever we go next, however long we dance around the kitchen for, I will always be able to say that we showed each other how good love can really feel. And I will be grateful for that forever.

SEXUALITY

when something is too powerful
they call that thing a threat
the aim then, is to destabilise
make that thing forget
all that is innate and
wondrous and owed
all that is within
untakable and owned
the heist then, must be clean
covert, fingerprint free
the poison: untraceable
"the way it's always been"
smother us with shame
sneak fear under our skin
threaten us with exile
call it an evil thing
to know your own body
to feel all she feels
to follow where might be magic
to say no when it isn't real
to explore every pleasure
to expand, to be seen
to know what we desire
to want, and to eat.

COMING OUT

"When you come out, you should let me interview you for the magazine," said the woman lying next to me, who I was fast falling in love with. Morning light was drowsily making its way through my bedroom window, and we were doing our usual dance of avoiding the day so that we could stay curled together for as long as possible.

As flattered as I was that she thought I was worthy of a feature in the queer magazine she worked for, the first part of the sentence didn't sit quite right in my brain.

When you come out...

My alarm burst into the space between us before I could answer, and I peeled myself away to turn it off. I went back for one more kiss before rolling out of bed and plodding across my cold wooden floor in search of caffeine. I thought about what she'd said, and whether I was planning on coming out any more than I already had.

It was true that I hadn't made any major public declaration of my sexual orientation, but more and more, I was wondering whether I needed to. I didn't see myself as 'in' any kind of closet. I was just... existing.

I'd been exploring my sexuality for a few years, dating across the gender spectrum and coming to terms with the fact that I wasn't as straight as I'd believed myself to be for most of my life. I'd come out to my friends and family, and I'd made passing comments about my dating life online, but I'd stopped short of an official announcement of my queerness. I had mixed feelings about making it into a big thing when maybe, it didn't need to be...

On the one hand, I've shared *so* much of my private life online over the years, and I know I don't *owe* the details of my sexuality to anyone. But on the other hand, I also know how important it still is to see positive representations of queerness. I know, because I grew up with so few.

My earliest memory of someone coming out is from 2002. I was nine years old and Will Young had just won *Pop Idol* – a win that was fast eclipsed by the tabloid circus of him announcing his queerness. I remember seeing the inky front pages of newspapers emblazoned with the words "I'M GAY" and days of entertainment reporters talking about nothing else. The same year, *Top of the Pops* chose not to air the music video for t.A.T.u.'s number one single 'All the Things She Said', which famously showed the two teenage girls kissing. I decided at the time that I didn't think there was anything *wrong* with being gay, but clearly, it was a very big deal...

I went through primary school whilst Section 28 – a law in the UK that banned schools from teaching "the acceptability of homosexuality" – was still being enforced.[13] This meant that there were no Pride flags in our classrooms or books that celebrated different kinds of families. Relationships outside of the hetero-normative just weren't mentioned. Section 28 was finally repealed in 2003, but the social undercurrent of homophobia in my small hometown only seemed to get stronger as we aged.

By the time I'd reached secondary school, the word 'gay' was the most commonly heard insult down every hallway. Homophobic bullying was *everywhere* – there was even a section of the playground that had been dubbed 'the gay circle' – if you stepped into it, you were immediately harassed by the popular kids who waited nearby. We all skirted round the area, scared of forgetting and overstepping the line.

It was the boys who faced the majority of the abuse for doing anything that could be perceived as gay. Girls who didn't fit the expected standard of femininity were teased about being lesbians, but the general consensus was that women couldn't *really* be gay. If a girl wasn't interested in a boy, she was probably just frigid.

As we got older, the idea of women being with other women was more accepted, but only ever in the context of fulfilling a male fantasy. Lesbians were welcome! As long as they were hot and hyper-sexual and there to please whichever man was watching. Queer women still didn't *really* exist outside of the straight male gaze.

Against a backdrop of homophobia and the erasure of queer women, I never seriously questioned whether I was anything other than straight. I liked boys. In fact, I liked them obsessively.

I wrote anthologies of love letters to the boys I liked. I scribbled their initials on every notebook I owned. I studied their behaviour like an insatiable anthropologist. I once stormed out of my best friend's house when I was nine years old because she dared to suggest that the boy

I'd been enamoured with for the past two years *might* not be my future husband.

And of course, I was obsessed! One of these boys was going to be my Prince Charming! The one who would swoop in and make my life complete. That's what every depiction of love had ever shown me, and if I got things right, that fairytale could be mine, too!

I moved from being deeply invested in the Prince Charming fairytale to being deeply invested in securing sexual validation from men during my teenage years. The goal was still being chosen. If I was chosen, then I was getting it right – 'it' meaning womanhood within patriarchy.

During those teenage years, the thrill of being chosen felt like butterflies and sweaty palms and warmth all over my body. At times, I think I conflated the chemical rush of male validation for attraction itself. That's not to say there wasn't attraction mixed in there, but when it's coupled with the affirmation that you're getting it right, you're desirable enough, you're winning at womanhood! That's one hell of a drug.

And because I was so invested in getting womanhood right, the idea of being with another woman just didn't feel like a valid option.

I would happily kiss a woman on a night out – but only when a man was present, so that I could tell myself we were doing it for his gaze.

I would spend hours poring over imagery of women's bodies – but only telling myself that I wanted to *be* her, not that I could possibly want to be *with* her.

I would find myself fantasising about being with women while my boyfriend tried to get me off – but I told myself that everyone thinks about that during sex. Nothing gay to see here!

In hindsight, there were plenty of clues that my sexuality existed somewhere more in the middle of the spectrum than I was telling myself. But I couldn't open myself up to that possibility. I was straight, and that was the end of the story.

I don't think I could have seen myself as anything other than straight until I did a whole lot of divesting from the patriarchal idea of successful womanhood.

* * *

When I finally arrived at the possibility of my own queerness, it felt like I was late to the party.

I was only twenty-seven, but it seemed like everyone else had been openly exploring their sexuality for years! By my own imaginary schedule, I was behind, which only contributed to the feelings of imposter-syndrome that crept in every time I considered saying out loud that I might not be straight. My brain was filled with every invalidating counter-point imaginable:

How can you be queer if you've only ever dated men?

What if you've just convinced yourself that you're queer to sound cool?

You don't look very queer...

You shouldn't be taking up space that doesn't belong to you.

You'll never experience the oppression that genuinely queer people have had to face, so why should you get to be part of the queer community?

My personal brand of overthinking when it came to my sexuality had a distinctly internet flavour to it. Social media is overrun with gatekeepers ready to tell you exactly what queerness is, exactly what you should call yourself, exactly what you're allowed to do and what you're not. In many of the moments that I'd considered publicly discussing my sexuality over the years, the internalised audience in my mind would sing with reasons why I was wrong and bad and didn't belong.

Even for people who are navigating their sexuality without an audience, the expectation to know exactly who you are and be ready to explain it to other people can be stifling. Sometimes it feels as if you have to prepare a fully researched thesis on your own sexuality and present it to a board of strangers before you're allowed to claim part of your own identity.

Dating and sex are meant to be exciting, explorative, revealing. We're meant to learn things about ourselves as we go. The pressure to present a perfectly figured-out version of ourselves can steal that joy before it's even had a chance to be felt. I knew that before I made any decisions about publicly coming out I needed at least a bit of time to figure things out for myself, and to explore.

I was pretty sure that I found people of all genders attractive, but did that mean I wanted to date them? Was I bi or was it just normal for straight women to fantasise about being with other women? And what was the difference between bisexual and pansexual? Could I really see myself as... queer?

There was so much I didn't know. But at least for a while, I didn't need to.

I didn't need to quickly pick a label.

I didn't need to justify the feelings I was just starting to accept.

I didn't need to give part of my identity away for other people's judgement before I'd properly had a chance to settle into it myself.

I could just... be.

I could open up the genders on my dating profile. I could flirt with him, and her, and them. I could explore my attraction with an open mind and let myself enjoy the moment. And I was allowed to take my time – I wasn't behind, I was right on schedule.

* * *

After a few dates, a few queer community events and a whole lot of self-reflection, I decided that it was time to come out to the people I was closest to. Most of my friends were already aware that I'd been exploring – some of them were surprised, some of them were curious, but all of them were one hundred percent supportive (and my queer friends were just excited that I was joining the team). That only left family.

I joined my mum on the daily dog walk that we'd done together hundreds of times before. We trudged down familiar pathways, commenting on the same scenery and falling into comfortable quiet. Halfway round our usual route, I told her that I'd been out with someone and by the way, that someone happened to be a woman.

"Oh, branching out?" she said cheerfully as we marched along.

"Something like that..." I replied, swerving a persistent patch of brambles.

"As long as you're happy, my dear." She smiled and we carried on, a little bit different but exactly the same.

My dad, brother and sister were all equal parts accepting and unbothered. I am exceptionally lucky to be surrounded by people whose love for me doesn't depend on who I love or how I identify. It's the kind of acceptance that every queer person deserves to feel from their family, but that so many still don't get.

That just left the question of how I wanted to navigate coming out online. I was torn.

Part of me didn't understand why I should make a big deal out of something that *shouldn't* be a big deal. So I was attracted to people other than cis men – so what? Weren't we moving away from the time of people having to make statements about their sexuality?

'Coming out' only exists as a concept because we've designated everyone straight by default. Compulsory heterosexuality positions straightness as the only viable option, something that we have to actively *opt out of* because our participation has been taken for granted in the first place. Why should I have to turn part of my identity into a statement just because the world assumes that everyone's straight? I don't *owe* an explanation of my sexuality to anyone.

But I also can't ignore how much of a privilege it is to exist in a time and place where I'm able to come out without the overwhelming fear of rejection, abuse or scandal that so many queer people before me have had to face. Not too long ago – within my lifetime – a young, white, cisgender pop star announcing that he was gay had still been front page news. A lot has changed since then. A lot of LGBTQ+ activists have fought tirelessly for things to change, and for my experience of coming out to be different.

Gay marriage has only been legal in England and Wales since 2013, in the US – across all fifty states – since 2015 and in Australia and Northern Ireland, only since 2017 and 2020 respectively.[14] There are still sixty-four countries with laws that criminalise homosexuality, twelve of which allow the death penalty as a punishment for same-sex sexual activity.[15] And even though the UK has become a generally more accepting place for people who identify as gay, lesbian or bisexual, the trans community are still consistent targets of dehumanising public debate, with newspapers, politicians and prominent celebrity figures spreading transphobic hatred and misinformation. In 2023, hate crimes against transgender people reached a record high.[16] Things might be better for some of us, but true equality means things being better for *all of us*.

So, even though me coming out as queer might not be the biggest deal, and even though it isn't owed, I still decided that I wanted to share that part of myself publicly. The value of sharing outweighed any reservations I had.

I didn't make a major statement, I just started being a bit more open in what I was sharing. I spoke about going to queer events; I mentioned that I was dating people of all genders; I started gradually referring to myself as queer. I came out bit by bit, in my own way.

When I was ready, I told my followers that I'd been dating someone new – and she was incredible. I was proud to be with her. As far as labels go, pansexual is probably the most accurate, since my attraction to people doesn't depend on gender or body parts, it depends on the person. But bisexual, meaning that I'm attracted to more than one gender, is fine too.

There was a small amount of negativity, but the love outweighed the hate by a landslide.

I hope that we are moving towards a time when coming out doesn't have to be a big deal, for anyone. And maybe one day it won't even be necessary – maybe we'll stop assuming that everyone fits into one category by default and embrace how gloriously different we all are. But until we get there, there are a few things that every queer person should know about coming out:

There is no right or wrong way to come out, there is only *your* way. However long it takes, however loudly or quietly it happens, your identity is yours to share or not share as you decide.

Your safety and well-being are the most important things, always. If it isn't safe for you to come out, you don't have to. You are still valid in your identity, and you still belong in the queer community.

You are loved. Even if it doesn't feel like it at times, there will be places that accept you, and people who embrace you for exactly who you are. Keep going, and you'll find them.

As for me, coming out is one more way that I've come home to myself; another piece of who I am that I've found, accepted, and welcomed back into the whole. One more step towards being my biggest, most unapologetic self, proudly.

WHAT FEELS GOOD

Content warning: contains discussion of FGM

"You just... keep going," she said, cigarette in hand, the grey waves of the coastline crashing behind her.

I glanced around the sandswept shelter, triple-checking that we were still the only ones there. We'd come to the place we usually did when it was time to do things that parents don't want to see and speak about things that parents don't want to hear.

Smoking and sex talk were the only two items on the agenda when we met up after school and giggled our way down to the beach.

We'd been best friends once before, when we were very young and I was enthralled by the yellow of her hair. But we'd left that friendship at the gates of primary school, both moving on to new groups and different priorities. For a few years we'd only exchanged a casual nod in the hallway when one clique passed another, but now we were back to holding each other's secrets and losing track of time sharing everything and nothing together.

"But how do you know where?" I let myself ask, begging the colour to stay out of my cheeks.

"You'll know," she said, revelling in her years of experience.

We'd both lost the rest of our friends at around the same time, for very different reasons. Mine had been scared away by the mental illness that starved my body and left me trapped inside myself. Hers had decided that she was a slut. Even though they were all having casual sex with each other, she'd suddenly overstepped the acceptable limit, and was cast out.

Somehow, we re-found each other: one who hadn't allowed herself any pleasure for years and another who'd apparently allowed herself too much.

We spent hours huddling by the beach in the dead of winter, her telling me all of the stories that got her banished and me lapping them up, ravenous.

I thought she was magic – so unapologetic, not a stroke of shame about her body or what it could do. I listened while she filled me in on every unimaginable detail, wondering what it might be like to invite that kind of feeling into my life, into my body.

I was convinced at that point that I'd fallen far behind the rest when it came to exploring those things. I'd lost years that should have been filled with awkward teenage fumbles and properly learning how to kiss to being sick, and I was more than keen to catch up.

I asked her what first times were like, and she laid out her impressive debut. I asked her exactly what you're supposed to say at which moment, and she gave me advice that made sense in our sixteen-year-old brains. I asked her what it feels like, *really*, and she promised that it's even better than when you do it by yourself.

That's where she lost me. My eyes darted to the salt spray bursting over the concrete sea wall.

I had no frame of reference for 'doing it by myself'. I knew what she was talking about, and I'd been curious enough to kind of, almost, nearly try a few times... but nothing had ever stuck. I hadn't hit any sacred spot or felt any mind-blowing sensation. I'd always stopped after a minute or so, sure that I just couldn't have any, or didn't know enough to find the ones that were in there.

Seagulls sleepily circled above. I decided to tell her that I'd never reached the promised land. If she was telling me every detail of her adventures, down to how different boys tasted, I could trust her to hold this.

"I've never... you know, I haven't..."

"You haven't come?"

"Yeah, never had an orgasm..." I shrugged off the enormity of the statement and half hoped that she was about to cry "Me neither!" and admit that every last detail of her flooded sex life had been made up. Instead, she looked genuinely confused.

I tried to explain that it wasn't because I saw anything wrong with it (although at that point, I was still hauling around suitcases worth of sexual shame), it just... didn't seem to work. I couldn't find the right thing to think about. I couldn't find the right rhythm to move in. And if I'd been more honest with her, I would have also shared that I couldn't shake the burning feeling that I was doing something wrong.

All of this made no sense to my friend. She'd stumbled across her own sacred spot years ago and hadn't left it alone since. As far as she was concerned, she'd found herself in a body that was capable of creating almost instant pleasure, why wouldn't she feel it?

She lit another cigarette (something else I hadn't tried), and walked me through exactly what to do.

"The first time does take a while," she offered with understanding. "You just... keep going."

"But how do you know where?"

"You'll know."

"What am I supposed to think about?" I asked, reaching the end of my vulnerability supply.

"I don't think about anything," she looked off into her recent memory, "I just focus on the feeling."

* * *

Later on, my patchwork collage walls and musty ornamental stuffed toys looked down as I set off, newly determined, to find something that felt good in my body. I wondered whether rooms really did hold histories of what happened inside them. If so, it was about time I offered up some pleasure to balance the amount of pain I'd felt in mine.

I opened my legs – but not too wide, in case I thought that I was desperate – and allowed my hand to linger over the areas I was still embarrassed to name out loud. I tried to move my fingers in a way that felt good, but all I felt for a good while was wrong.

I shifted around, changed my speed, tried left-handed, went to find something to use as a lube, froze in panic every time I heard footsteps outside the room. The feeling of shame that began at the idea of what I was doing was joined by another layer: the shame of not even being able to do it right.

Why did I need to do this anyway? I was fine as I was, staying as detached as I could from my body and her feelings. My hand flopped down to my side, ready to call it a night.

I remembered how my friend had looked earlier that day, the aura of adulthood that oozed around her when she spoke. Like she had figured out a trick that we weren't meant to know yet, and now she had it, it couldn't be taken away. I wanted that. I wanted to feel like I had something, here in this body that I'd been trying to make disappear for so long.

I remembered what she said – *the first time does take a while, just focus on the feeling...*

Five more minutes, I told myself, *five more minutes and we can give up.* And since I was so close to giving up anyway, I stopped caring so much about whether I was going to get there. The tension left my body, and I tapped into a natural rhythm. After a couple of minutes, something happened. Something started to feel... good.

My brain seemed to zoom out and out in an infinite loop of everything growing smaller as the spark in my hand took on new life. I didn't want to take a breath in case I scared it away. *Keep going,* my brain said, *it's fine, it's no big deal, nothing to see here...*

When the wave came I was sure that I was about to be sick, or faint, or both. It was like my brain short-circuited to create a feeling so far outside of anything I'd ever known. I crash landed somewhere between awe and repulsion. I'd done it. My body had invited me to feel pure pleasure, and I'd let her.

It was a reconnection to something I'd buried long ago: the fact that she is me, and I am her, and we are here, together.

I smiled softly, nuzzling my face into my pillow and granting my brain permission to switch off for the day. We had found something sacred. We had felt good.

* * *

There are endless layers of engrained sexual shame for women to unlearn before we're able to fully embrace feeling good in our own bodies. Despite the fact that we've evolved with infinite potential for sexual pleasure, we have been strategically disconnected from our sexual selves, from knowing that we are the rightful owners of these bodies, and all that they can feel.

A 2023 study conducted by the menstrual healthcare company *Flo* found that 25% of women aged 18–34 *still* believe that masturbation is shameful.[17] Despite the leaps we've made with sex positivity in mainstream consciousness, too many of us still feel ashamed about a perfectly natural form of self-exploration. And when we look back at the ways that women's sexuality has been demonised and stigmatised throughout history, it makes complete sense why so many of us are still carrying that shame.

Under patriarchy, our sexuality has always been a problem. In Ancient Rome, whilst it was common and acceptable for men to have sexual partners outside of their marriages, women found guilty of adultery would be publicly shamed, exiled or killed.[18] Between the fifteenth and the eighteenth century, when tens of thousands of women were trialled, tortured and executed on suspicion of witchcraft, it was their supposedly demonic sexual habits that 'proved' their guilt.[19] And let's not forget how Eve was painted as a sinful seductress for convincing Adam to eat that fruit, a tale interpreted for centuries as an allegory for the danger of women giving into sexual temptation and corrupting men on the way.

When it comes to solo sex in particular, it was the Victorians who really doubled down on the idea that pleasuring yourself was not only unacceptable, but dangerous.[20] Masturbation was referred to as 'self-pollution' – a sin that would lead women to insanity, infertility and even death.

Treatment to prevent women pleasuring themselves too much included ice-cold baths, diets of plain foods, corsets that restricted access to the vulva and, in extreme cases, clitoridectomies: the surgical removal of the clitoris. And if that sounds like a barbaric historical practice, bear in mind that over 200 million women and girls alive today have been subjected to female genital mutilation (FGM): the practice of cutting the genitals so that a woman can adhere to cultural and religious standards of purity, and be more desirable to men.[21]

Is it any wonder that we're weighed down with shame when it comes to our sexual selves? Even now, sex education in schools is severely lacking in information on female pleasure, and Republican politicians in the US continue to push for restrictions on reproductive healthcare: a clear message that our bodily autonomy and sexual freedom can be revoked under patriarchy at any point.

We have to ask ourselves *why* there has been such a sustained and violent effort to suppress our sexuality for so long. Why have we been policed, blamed and punished for millennia, simply for being whole human beings with desires and urges like any other? The only plausible answer is that a woman who unapologetically claims her own sexuality is very dangerous indeed. She is a threat.

A woman who realises how much pleasure she can give herself, without needing to perform desirability, secure male validation or rely on anyone else is a threat to the patriarchal (and hetero-normative) narrative that men are necessary for us to feel good.

A woman who secures the physiological benefits of having regular orgasms – improved mood, better sleep and pain relief to name a few – is bound to be healthier and happier within herself, making her less profitable to a capitalist system that leverages our discontent to continually sell us things we don't need.

And a woman who refuses to conform to cultural norms, despite the threat of social shame, is so much harder to control. It's the fear of shame that keeps people in line. It taps into our tribal need to be seen as valuable by our social group in order to secure their protection. If we're perceived to be doing something shameful, our community might cast us out, leaving us open to dangers that we're unequipped to handle by ourselves. Our instincts tell us that we need to avoid social shame in order to stay safe, making the threat of shame one of the most effective tools for getting people to conform.

A woman who isn't scared of being shamed is uncontrollable. And that is a terrifying thing. If we are not under control, we might realise all the ways that we are still not treated equally, and we might demand more. On the other hand, if a culture can successfully shame a woman into detaching from something as innate as her own body and the pleasure it can feel, then she can be shamed into believing anything, even her own inferiority.

* * *

We are separated from our bodies over and over throughout our lives.

Diet culture teaches us to ignore our hunger, the most fundamental instinct we are born with. Purity culture teaches us to be ashamed of our capacity and desire for sexual pleasure. Hustle culture and the normalisation of hyper-productivity teaches us to push past our physical limits and our need for rest. With every wedge driven between ourselves and our bodies, we're promised a pay-off that will outweigh all of our sacrifice.

If we deny ourselves the simple pleasure of enjoying food, it will lead to a body that will feel better than anything we could taste.

If we say no to sexual exploration for long enough, it will give us a sense of moral goodness and societal approval that feels better than any orgasm could.

If we work tirelessly to squeeze productivity from every available second of the day, we'll end up with a feeling of accomplishment ten times better than the feeling of allowing ourselves to rest.

Then we wonder, when we've successfully torn ourselves away from our bodies and all of the ways they try to communicate with us, why we *still* don't feel good...

In my dieting years, I was always proud of how adamantly I could ignore my body. Hunger signals were something to block out, rather than the way my body was trying to express her need for energy. Injuries from endless workouts were things to push through, rather than my body screaming her need for rest.

As far as I was concerned, it was me versus my body. Only one of us could be in charge, and the other just had to be drowned out with rules and threats and punishment. Those years could probably better be described as the ones I spent trying to get as far away from my body as possible.

I believed, like so many of us do, that the reward would be worth it. That every bit of self-denial and each ignored need was leading me closer to the holy grail of the perfect body. And nothing would feel better than that. Nothing would feel better than catching a stranger's admiration in the street like fairy dust, wearing clothing with a single digit on the size label, looking in the mirror and seeing what I'd seen celebrated all my life.

But the longer I spent trying to break away from my own body, the more impossible it became to feel *anything* good, even as my outside got closer and closer to the goal. I kept expecting to wake up one day and feel peaceful in my body, connected and at-home. But what I was doing every day was reinforcing the opposite: that I needed to be completely disconnected, and override every feeling my body was trying to communicate to me. She couldn't possibly know what she needed. I knew better.

We reject the wisdom of our bodies as if bodies haven't been intelligent enough to survive millions of years of changing circumstances, adapt and evolve and keep us safe. We detach from what our own bodies attempt to tell us so that we can keep up with expectations – of beauty, of productivity, of who we should be. We listen to everything outside of us far more than we listen to what's coming from within.

If we want to be our most healed and whole selves, we must come home to our bodies. We have to uncover all of the ways we've been convinced to separate from our physical selves, remove the shame that keeps the wedge in place, and welcome all we can feel back into our lives. We have to recognise how much power and wisdom we have always held right here in our own skin – we were just tricked into letting it go.

It is a privilege to be here, in this body. She carries me. She keeps me safe. She works tirelessly to hold me, despite how hard I've tried to get away from her. She does everything she can to allow me to experience this life. The least I can do is let in what feels good. The least I can do is be here, with her.

SLUTHOOD

Content warning: contains discussion of sexual violence

I never had 'the talk'. There was never a moment when my parents sat me down and explained where babies come from, or what might start happening to my body leading up to the teenage years. There were things we just didn't mention.

On the night of my thirteenth birthday, when my period first arrived, I hovered anxiously outside their bedroom door, shrouded in shame and not knowing what to do. What was I supposed to say? Which words were the least embarrassing? What if I tried to tell my mum but my dad overheard and was horrified? What if he thought I was disgusting? *I* thought I was disgusting...

The things that bodies do weren't discussed. We just got on with life around them, as if they were inconveniences to pay no attention to. I stumbled into adolescence knowing nothing about sex, pleasure or the body parts involved.

Any information I had was gathered together from scraps of imagery I shouldn't have seen. One evening I was allowed to stay up later than usual to watch a period drama with lots of corsets and horses and talk about duty. I sat next to my mother in burning silence, watching what I gathered to be sex, wondering why I was intrigued and repulsed at the same time.

I got the message that sex was secretive, and wrong, and not something that good girls are curious about. Boys, on the other hand, seemed to know all about it.

I was eight years old when a boy from my class started making sexually explicit comments about wanting to touch me and show me things. He told crude jokes that he said he'd learned from his dad. It only stopped after a meeting involving my parents.

I was eleven years old when I started secondary school and sat listening to the boys in my history class bragging about the things they'd watched on the internet when their parents weren't looking. "Have any of you done a blowjob before?" they asked us, unashamed, "It's not even worth bothering unless you know how to deepthroat."

I was twelve years old when the older boy from my swimming club started telling me how sexy he thought I was. How even though he had a girlfriend, he really wanted to take my virginity. He knocked on my door one afternoon to walk me down to the sports centre like a gentleman. Just before we got there he turned, leant over, pushed his tongue into my mouth and moved it around for what felt like hours. Then he told me he had a boner. I wasn't sure whether I'd done something right or wrong.

By the time sex education was covered in school, there were already countless rumours about people who had lost it in all kinds of places (apparently one girl did it in an inflatable boat out at sea, for privacy). A woman in her sixties with a constantly displeased expression showed us how to fit a banana with a condom, and told us to save our first time for something special, and not a "Quick shag in a shed."

We learned nothing about consent, or pleasure, or queer sex. We left the classroom embarrassed on behalf of a banana and carried on trying to source our own information: a magazine article here, a story from an older sibling there.

There was one girl in my friendship group who knew more than the rest of us combined. After we'd finished singing along to Disney songs at a sleepover, she showed us the hair she had growing, and told us what she knew about how you're supposed to touch a boy's thing. We couldn't stop talking about who was going to do it first, how it might feel, what it meant. Would it make us a slut? Not unless everybody found out.

The girls who were labelled as sluts were the ones who were unfortunate enough to have done their exploring with a boy who cared more about cashing in on his new social capital than keeping whatever had happened between them private. Those girls were pushed out, ignored and shamed by the ones who were doing exactly the same things, but managing to keep it a secret.

By the time everyone else had started their fumbling experimental years, I was out of the game. You lose a lot when you spend your early teenage years too unwell to be part of life. Whilst I was in hospital battling against an eating disorder, my friends were staying up late playing truth or dare and meeting their first boyfriends in the field across from school. I knew I had to get back to them, and catch up.

My first experience came during one of the big group sleepovers I'd heard so much about. There were eight of us, an even split of boys and girls all squished together on the floor of a teenage bedroom. We'd been watching movies, eating pizza and sharing secrets and when the evening wound down, I found myself lying next to a boy who I'd never paid much attention to before.

As far as I was aware, the boy didn't have any feelings for me, and I didn't have any for him. But he was kind, and shy, and when we were the last two people left awake, awkwardly sharing one duvet, he gently guided my hand down to where he wanted me to touch, and then touched me in return. No words, before, during or after.

The experience in itself was underwhelming and stressful. I spent the whole time worrying whether I was doing it right and what he might be thinking. *Should I have shaved before this? How much pressure am I supposed to be using? How do I know when it's over? Do we just keep going until we get tired? What do we do after?* I had so many questions but I was sure that asking them would kill the moment. Besides, he probably didn't know the answers either.

I kept moving my hand in what I guessed was the correct way. His breathing quickened and he seemed less and less focused on whatever his fingers were meant to be doing to me, then after a grunt and a dribble of something warm and wet, he pulled away and stopped moving altogether. *Was that it? What was I meant to do now? Should I go and wash my hand? Do we just go to sleep?* He still wasn't saying anything... *Did I do something wrong?*

I was too scared to manoeuvre myself to the bathroom, so I wiped the stickiness off on the nearest bit of material and pretended to go to sleep, replaying the whole confusing thing over and over until daylight crept into the room. I didn't know how I was supposed to interact with the boy in the morning, but I knew that I had to tell the girls absolutely *everything*.

We waited for the boys to leave, off to their football practices and family lunches, then we huddled like a coven of witches, a bag of Maltesers as our cauldron. No detail was left undevoured: *how big? For how long? Who initiated? Was it good? Did he say anything? Was he good? Did you orgasm? Did he? What did you do with it? Euuwwww!*

Sex gossip was the most exciting thing we'd ever had to share. There we were, exploring a whole new world of feelings, together. We were suddenly so worldly, so mature, surely the first girls to ever discover these things! Oversharing our encounters became a ritual, each of us taking turns lapping up the curiosity and praise and shock.

Within the space of a year, I went from never having been touched, to regularly having casual sex after house parties and nights out. I'd also been introduced to drinking, and the two experiences seemed to go hand in hand. Whenever one of us managed to get hold of alcohol, there was a possibility for the evening to end with a different person in a different bed, and the thrill of it was intoxicating.

One of my friends was the girl with all the experience, and she lauded her encounters over me like they were medals I had yet to win. But I'm quite competitive, and I learn fast.

We would go on nights out together, pre-drinking whatever we could get hold of in large quantities so we were drunk enough to not need another throughout the night. Numb to the cold and overly confident, we set out to secure our next experience, and the validation that came with it. She kissed two guys in one night, I kissed three. She got the bartender's phone number, and I found someone outside the bar. She got with the guy from our English class, I went for the one in Maths.

We collected up every lurid detail and pored over them like archaeologists at an excavation site. We kept a tally of our encounters, gently teasing about who was in the lead. We were sluts, but we owned it. Being careless with our bodies was what we were meant to do at our age! Why were other people so uptight about it? They all wanted to be doing it, really.

I basked in having come so far from being the sick girl who was left behind to now, being sexually confident and accomplished and ahead of the curve. Was I enjoying the sex that I was having? It's hard to say... I enjoyed the validation. I enjoyed being wanted. I enjoyed playing the game. But all the sex I was having was performative, detached, focused entirely on what they wanted and trying to avoid my own devastating body insecurities.

We saw ourselves as empowered, grown women. And it was empowering, in a way. It was empowering to break away from the sexual shame and culture of silence that had been passed down to us. It was empowering to boldly initiate the encounters instead of sitting back and believing that nobody would be interested. It was empowering to explore ourselves outside of those encounters, because along with encouraging each other to have sex with other people, we also encouraged each other to explore ourselves sexually, buying our first toys together and sharing tips and tricks.

But there were layers to what we were doing that weren't empowering at all, at least not for me. Every night out started in the afternoon, with a full body scrub and shave, a skipped dinner, a long make-up routine, uncomfortable shapewear and hours of sucking in. The version of myself that I felt I had to embody in order to harness sexual attention wasn't really me at all. Nor was the version of myself that showed up in bed with these people.

The sex I was having wasn't freeing or exploratory or even safe, most of the time. It followed the hetero-normative porn script of focusing on their pleasure whilst making myself as small and unimposing as possible. It was making the right noises at the right times but never allowing myself to truly be in the moment. It didn't matter if I finished or even really started – I was a thing they were doing sex to, rather than a person they were having sex with. And in the haze of girlish giggles and fun gossiping that came afterwards, it was safer to ignore the fact that sometimes we didn't actually want it to happen the way it did.

Sometimes, we only really wanted a bit of flirtation and maybe a kiss, but we didn't have the words to stop the ball once it was rolling. Sometimes, the whole thing got uncomfortable and awkward and we would have rather left, but what if the guy got annoyed? Sometimes, we actually did say no, more than once, but they either didn't hear us or didn't want to. So we laughed about it the next morning and told ourselves that we were empowered, grown women, because if we didn't, we would have had to face things that we didn't know how to face.

The conversation around consent is unrecognisable today compared to what it was when we started having sex. There was no awareness that a true 'yes' should be enthusiastic, informed and sober. There was no talk of boundaries or examples of how you might ask someone what they like. Back then, the general consensus was that anything other than a screaming no was essentially a yes, and as a result, every single woman I know has had experiences that sit in a grey area that we don't know how to name. Or maybe we do know, but it's too confronting to say out loud.

Towards the end of my teenage sluthood, I found myself at a house party with some of the usual crowd plus a few new faces. I was nervous about being there because I was trying to repair my friendship with the person whose house it was, after we'd drifted apart throughout my illness. I decided, early on in the night, that I wasn't feeling sexual and that I might even go home early – I only lived a short walk away.

Throughout the evening, one boy was particularly persistent with his flirtation. He'd obviously been told that me and my friend were up for having fun, and he assumed that he'd easily get what he wanted. He subtly followed me around, asking if I wanted to go outside with him, somewhere private. I said I didn't think so, making sure I still appeared to be flattered and shy and all the other things we're told to be to not hurt the male ego. He set about convincing me to change my mind as if it were a mission he'd been sent on by some greater power.

He started with politeness and 'Please, please'. I held my ground and left the conversation as soon as I could. He showed up again and changed his tactic to using guilt – 'come on,' he said, 'I really want this'. I tried to find another variation of saying no, softly, and latched onto a friend who walked past as a way to get out.

At this point, my defences felt worn. I was not well practised at saying no, to anything. I was raised to be a people pleaser who didn't let people down and certainly didn't have boundaries around my own wants and needs. Saying no, in any situation, was painfully difficult. It made me feel selfish, like a bad person, like an inconvenience to everyone else.

I told another friend that this guy was being really persistent, but I didn't want anything to happen. She said she understood and that I could stick with her for the rest of the night, but she fell asleep soon after, and I didn't know where to go. I should have gone home.

The next time I passed by the boy with his group of friends in the kitchen, he pulled me outside by the arm and started kissing me before I had the chance to speak. I didn't want to make a scene by trying to run away, so I let him, hoping that was all he would do and then I would be able to leave. It wasn't all he did. Without a word, he unbuttoned his jeans, lifted my leg, and tried to find his way inside me. I blocked him with my hands, telling myself that maybe I could just get away with giving him a quick handjob... besides, he was so drunk he probably wouldn't know the difference.

He thrusted against me for a while, pausing every so often to say how good it felt. I suppose I was meant to be flattered, but I mainly just wanted it to stop. And it did. He pulled away, put himself back inside his trousers, and took my hand, leading me into the kitchen where his friends were still standing. They jeered as we entered, congratulating the boy on his seemingly successful mission. I smiled as I was meant to, and said that I was going to sleep in the other room with a friend. Suddenly, the air in the room shifted.

'No no no, you can't go to bed yet,' one of the boys said. 'You haven't even tried this!' He held out a bottle of coconut rum. I'd been drinking a little bit but by that point I felt near enough sober.

'Oh, I don't like coconut,' I said meekly.

'Just try it,' the boy said, pushing the bottle towards me.

'It doesn't even taste like coconut, trust me.'

The bottle was nearly empty and I thought, how bad could it be? The three of them all started encouraging me, telling me to just have a little bit, it was really good, honestly, I'd really like it. I took the bottle, swigged, and swallowed down the immediate urge to be sick.

'One more,' they said, and I obliged. It didn't cross my mind that they could have added something else to the drink.

The next part of the night is completely blank. Erased entirely from my mind. I don't know how much time passed, what was said or what was done to me before I came to, completely naked in my friend's hot tub with all three of the boys and the girl who was my usual partner in sluthood.

I was on top of a boy I'd barely spoken to before and had no interest in. He was telling the other boys to watch how good I was as he pushed my head under the water towards his crotch. I came up spluttering, trying to act like everything was normal and like I knew what was going on.

Of course, my brain filled in the gaps, *we got way too drunk and ended up having an orgy! That's exactly something we would do. Haha!* The boys continued to pass us around. I didn't know how drunk my friend was but she was giggling away, performing her favourite tricks, seemingly having a great time. I took her lead and acted like I was, too.

In the early hours of the morning, we walked home together, hair dripping onto the pavement. I felt sick and my body ached. I wanted my bed and to never have to interact with anyone ever again. We tried to tap into our usual post-escapade gossip. *Who do you think was the best? What is everyone at school gonna think? Oh my god, I can't believe we did that!*

When we got in, I crawled under the covers and tried to think about anything other than what had just happened. The hangover the next day was worse than any I'd felt before. I felt covered in thick disgust, barely able to move my limbs through the heaviness of it. I couldn't eat much and I kept trying to piece together the parts of the night that I couldn't remember, but they just weren't there. I'd gone from being fully conscious of my surroundings to blacked-out, but I couldn't bring myself to question whether my drink had been spiked.

I met my friend the next morning and we walked together, bracing ourselves for the gossip to slither around the school. She was her usual, unashamed self, proud of her adventurousness and happy to add a few fresh notches to her post. Her narrative felt much more comfortable than exploring any alternative, so I repeated it to myself and everyone else until it felt like the whole truth: *We were so drunk! We had an orgy in a hot tub! Yep, it's true! Hahaha!*

Life carried on. I started dating my first long-term partner and closed the chapter of my teenage sluthood. I placed that night in its own little box in the back of my mind where it faded, untouched, until it started to feel like it had happened to someone else entirely, and not me at all.

Ten years later, the internet is exploding with women's' lived experience of sexual assault and harassment. You can't look anywhere without seeing #MeToo. Every time I go online I'm invited to share my own experiences to add to our collective voice.

I gaze back into the past, reframing all of the moments that never felt quite right. I remember countless instances of being objectified and fetishised. I remember being grabbed and groped in busy places and looking up to not be sure which passing man had done it. I remember being dragged outside of clubs by men I'd spoken a few words to and running back after realising how unsafe I was.

I try to reconcile the fact that yes, I had been embracing sluthood over those years, but there were still lines that had been crossed. Just because I'd been promiscuous didn't mean that consent and communication and basic respect should have been out the window. If anything, those things should have been *more* present. But my mind still lingers on the idea that maybe I'd deserved some of the things that happened. Maybe I'd brought them on myself...

As I reflect, my brain does backflips to avoid opening the box that contains the memory of that night, and the drink. *It's been settled. It was so long ago. Can I even trust what I remember? It can't have been that... I'm probably wrong.*

My boyfriend at the time worked in construction, and he moved around to different building sites quite a lot. At one point he started a new job and came home late, telling me about all the lads in the crew and who he was getting along with. One of the names he mentioned sent an electric shock through my brain. It was the guy from that night. The one who wouldn't accept my no.

I knew I had to tell my boyfriend what had happened, but I still didn't know what to call it. I said something about having had a bad experience with the guy, that he'd pressured me into doing things with him that I didn't want to do. Apparently the two of them had a talk about it the next day, ending in a manly handshake and a continued comradery onsite. I avoided picking my boyfriend up from work, afraid to cross paths with the blurry figure from my past. I worried what he might be saying to my boyfriend, what he might paint me out to be.

Sporadically, I'd have flashbacks. Tasting coconut. Choking on water. The eyes of the boys standing around me, hungry. It took another few years for me to fully admit what had happened, and say it out loud. I had so many questions, like where do seventeen-year-old boys in small towns get hold of date rape drugs? Had they given it to my friend, too? Do they understand what they did? Are they sorry? Did they ever admit to themselves that it was rape? I hadn't admitted it to myself for so long...

And what does that make me, now? A survivor? What if I don't want that as part of my identity? What if I don't want to carry this with me, into new relationships, into the way I see myself and other people and sex? When someone physically takes you, without your consent, they take so much more than just your body in that moment.

It took me years of questioning, processing and learning how to see myself clearly before I could believe what I now know to be true: *of course* it was never my fault. *Of course* I hadn't brought it on myself. *Of course* I wasn't to blame. Even if I had been drinking. Even if I had been promiscuous before. Despite the fact that I hadn't kicked and screamed and gone home early. For women, it feels like there are so many layers of shame and misinformation to remove before we're allowed to say that the thing that happened to us was not okay. There is so much we experience that is not okay.

We are still told that it's up to us to cover up, watch our drink, don't smile unless you're interested (but also always *do* smile), make sure someone knows where you are, leave a fingerprint in the back of the taxi, walk a different way home, take a self-defence class, don't go out at night, don't be a tease (but also, don't be a prude), don't take nudes, don't stop to talk, don't go alone, let them down gently, don't hurt his ego, don't be cold (but don't be too warm), don't wear a short skirt or show too much skin, don't flirt, don't do anything at all, if you want to avoid getting hurt.

The thing is, we can tie ourselves into beautiful bows trying to follow all the rules of staying safe and it still will not guarantee our safety. Because ultimately, it's not down to us, and what we do and how we look and how we act, it's down to the men who believe they are entitled to our bodies, entitled to enact violence, entitled to take.

I wish there was half as much focus on raising boys to respect bodily autonomy and understand consent as there is on teaching girls how to protect themselves. I wish we didn't exist within a culture that normalises and minimises sexual violence to protect men who don't understand the word no. I wish we could make our sexual decisions without fear or shame – whether that means embracing sluthood or celibacy or anything in between.

We deserve to be able to explore and express ourselves sexually and still be safe. Still have our boundaries and our bodies respected. I don't regret those early days of sluthood, but I wish they had come from a place of knowledge and self-love, rather than desperately trying to catch up and collect validation. More than that, I wish that the culture around me could have been different, so that I could have explored safely.

Truly empowered sluthood is a wonderful thing. Women taking ownership of their bodies, releasing engrained shame, and prioritising their pleasure is beautiful. After centuries of sexist double standards and puritanical suppression, reclaiming our sexuality is the least we are owed. These are *our* bodies to move and feel and experience. Nobody should be able to take that away from us.

If I could go back and talk to my younger self, I might try to tell her that she doesn't have to be in such a rush. There is so much time to explore your sexual self, and it should never feel like a competition or a pressure to catch up.

I would tell her to focus on herself, first. Masturbate more, spend more time naked, with your own body. Learn to look in the mirror without zooming in on everything you've been conditioned to see as a flaw. Touch yourself softly – no more grabbing and poking the parts you don't like. Unlearn the idea that only certain bodies are desirable. Learn to see yourself as desirable, before seeking that validation from outside.

Understand that your body is yours, first and foremost and always. Nobody else is owed access to you. Practise saying no, to everything and anything that you don't want or like in life, so that when the time comes to share your body with someone else, you won't put their wants above your own.

Be a slut, if that's what feels empowering to you. But be safe. Educate yourself on STIs and protection and don't compromise your safety for some boy who says he doesn't like how condoms feel. If you don't feel comfortable enough with someone to tell them what you like, or ask when they last got tested, that's probably not someone you should be having sex with. Conversation comes before you get naked, always.

And no, the number of people you sleep with does not define your worth. But please know that you are worth something. You are not just a *thing* for other people to use and then discard. You are in charge of your body and what you do with it, and anyone who you choose to allow access to you should know how lucky they are.

One day, the sex will be better. And you'll feel able to show up as your real self, no more faking or performing. Until then, have fun. And don't be ashamed of a single thing.

THE SCRIPT

It took me ten years of having sex to be able to say anything while it was happening.

Don't get me wrong, it wasn't that I was *silent*. I'd watched enough porn and heard enough scripted moans of ecstasy to know which notes to hit and when.

But any vocal expression of myself – what I wanted, what I liked, how something actually felt – was locked away under layers of fear and shame. The idea of saying something – anything – during sex struck me with the kind of anxiety that's more likely to lead to a panic attack than an orgasm.

I believed that someone's sexual attraction to me was such a precarious thing that it could be squashed with a single misplaced remark. If I said something that wasn't sexy enough, used the wrong word, or the wrong tone at the wrong time, then I would be faced with certain rejection – tossed aside and discarded, unfit for use.

Nobody ever taught us, as we were racing towards our sexual starting lines, how *real* sex looks, feels or sounds. Our educators weren't educated enough to share the importance of prioritising pleasure, comfort and safe exploration. We weren't made aware of the many different forms that sex can take and still be valid, and enjoyable, and *good*.

Instead, we looked around us for examples of what sex was supposed to be, and took our scripts from wherever we could find them: unethical free porn sites, Hollywood films with adult ratings, magazine articles that told us the top ten ways to drive a man wild, gossip and rumours and tips passed down the grapevine.

The script for sex between a cis man and a cis woman always seemed to go the same way: a quick escalation that leads to penetration and ends whenever he does. There is no talk beforehand about protection, preferences or boundaries. Two people, often strangers, seamlessly and wordlessly fall into place, both knowing exactly what they're doing without any hesitation. No questions are asked. No laughter is shared. No awkwardness is felt. There are no breaks or deviations from the expected order of events.

Within this script, the role of the woman is clear: turn him on, make the right sounds while he does what he wants, be passive and satisfied with whatever you get.

By the time I was prepared to make my sexual debut, I had committed the script to memory like an actor ready for their starring role. I knew the noises and the poses. I knew the correct order of things. I knew how to make myself accommodating to almost anything he wanted. I knew when to open my mouth and when to keep it shut. I knew how to be 'good' at sex, according to everything I'd seen. The one thing I didn't know was how to keep hold of myself once the clothes were off.

In every sexual encounter, I performed as someone else: a woman with no reservations, no objections, no preferences and no needs. A woman with no voice.

I had sex for years without once being able to say "Could you move to the left a bit," or "Woah, not so hard." I communicated solely with body language and depth of breath, and even that felt bold! Too quick of a breathing pattern might have come across as being *too* into it, but too slow and he'd wonder if I was enjoying it at all... While I was busy monitoring my every breath, along with every angle of my body and how it might look to him, he was allowed to be there, in the moment, feeling it all without getting trapped in his own thoughts. I couldn't begin to imagine what that might be like.

Sometimes I'd have an urge – a phrase I wanted to hear or a position I wanted to try – and I'd feel my face prickle with heat just thinking about saying it out loud. Then I'd start panicking about how unattractive my face looks when it's red. Then I'd lose track of the performance entirely. I would have to doubly concentrate to stay on form until it was over. God forbid I ruin the experience for him.

I thought that I was having good sex. I was performing exactly as I was supposed to! Sure, I was never particularly present while the show was happening, but the other person always seemed to be enjoying themselves. It didn't matter if I had to bury my voice down and ignore my wants, as long as they were satisfied. At a core level, I believed that sex wasn't *for* me. It was only ever for them. The men.

Sex was something that I could provide for a man in exchange for the validation I got from him wanting it. I was a facilitator more than an active participant. My body was a thing for them to use, rather than part of my being that I could embody and direct for my own pleasure. My own pleasure was irrelevant; sex feeling good was sometimes a positive side effect, but it wasn't the point of the experience. The script ends with the man being completely satisfied, there is no mention of whether we are as well.

It is well known that the orgasm gap still exists between men and women. A 2022 YouGov survey found that only 30% of straight cis women reported always having an orgasm during sex, compared to 63% of straight cis men.[22] While reaching orgasm isn't the be all and end all of whether sex is enjoyable, the stats are a pretty clear indicator that women are not getting the pleasure they deserve. And I'm willing to bet that a large part of why is down to the scripts we're still using.

Any predetermined script for how sex should be is never going to work for all people, because all people are different. Our bodies are different, our brains are different, we've all had different experiences that shape our beliefs and how we feel about ourselves. There is no one-size-fits-all how-to guide to good sex – every sexual encounter is its own original experience that should be approached with curiosity and openness, not rules and expectations.

The cis-hetero normative script that so many of us pick up was simply not written with our pleasure in mind. In the script, women are usually objects, things to do sex *to* rather than people to have sex *with*. Our wants and needs aren't factored in because we aren't the protagonist of the situation, we are a means to someone else's end.

The script frames penetration as the only form of *real* sex. Reducing the definition of sex to the single act of a penis entering a vagina not only invalidates a lot of queer sexual experiences (which yes, absolutely count as sex), but it glosses over the fact that most people with vulvas need clitoral stimulation in order to reach the peak of sexual pleasure. Penetration isn't everything – if it was, there wouldn't be so many straight women still faking orgasms.

The script keeps us quiet, scared to say the wrong thing or breathe too heavily or shift position and ruin the moment. Because we are so consumed by how we are being perceived and whether we're measuring up to expectations, we cannot be present in our bodies and really *feel* what's happening, which blocks any chance of maxing out our pleasure. You have to be *in* your body to fully enjoy sex, not stuck in your own head.

Unsurprisingly, queer sex has higher rates of orgasm across the board. Without the cis-hetero normative script to follow, there is room to write something new, to get to know each others' bodies without preconceptions, to discover new kinds of pleasure, to mix up the order of things. Away from patriarchal power dynamics, you're also more likely to find mutual respect, and a belief that everyone's pleasure is equally important.

When I started having sex with people who weren't cis men, I went into each encounter unconsciously still following the same old script. I was ready to perform, to please them, to be whatever they wanted me to be! It quickly became clear that I didn't need to do any of those things, that there was a different way to approach sex that opened the possibility of it being good for *everyone*, not just the other person.

Don't get me wrong, you don't need to be queer to be having good sex (and not all queer sex is good!), but moving away from the cis-hetero normative script will make sex better for all of us, regardless of who we're sleeping with.

It's time for us to recognise how much better we deserve, and write ourselves a new set of guidelines for having good sex.

Let's start by normalising the idea that *really* good sex begins long before the clothes are off. It starts with everyone involved knowing themselves: what turns them on, what feels good, what doesn't feel good, what their boundaries are, and then being able to communicate all of that to the person or people they're going to have sex with.

The narrative that conversation kills the mood couldn't be more untrue. If you've ever been told exactly what your partner wants you to do to them and exactly how they want to make you feel, you know how much it can help to build anticipation and make the whole thing even better. Having a clear idea of your partner's desires and comfort levels is not only incredibly hot, it should be a baseline requirement before we even consider going any further.

And sure, ideally you don't want to be listening to someone's food shopping list while you're getting down to business (unless you have a shopping list kink, in which case, you do you boo), but checking in with each other throughout to see how everyone's feeling is something we should all be doing, especially if we're exploring the spicier stuff. We need to create sexual environments where it's okay to ask questions, take breaks or change your mind *at any point,* regardless of how far you've gone or if you think it'll ruin the moment. You are entitled to sex that feels safe, comfortable and informed from start to finish. Consent should always be ongoing.

Good sex can include laughter and moments of awkwardness. Bodies can be unpredictable, especially when you put two or more of them together! It's unrealistic to expect things to always be seamless; we are people, not futuristic sex robots.

There are no rules about the order you need to do things, where you need to reach or when it's time to stop. All of it is up to you, and whoever you're with. Forget about the script: improvise.

And if the old conditioning flares up, telling you to perform, to appease, to self-monitor, to not speak, recognise it for what it is: one more way we've been convinced to keep ourselves small. Let it try to hold you back all it wants, we don't follow old scripts anymore.

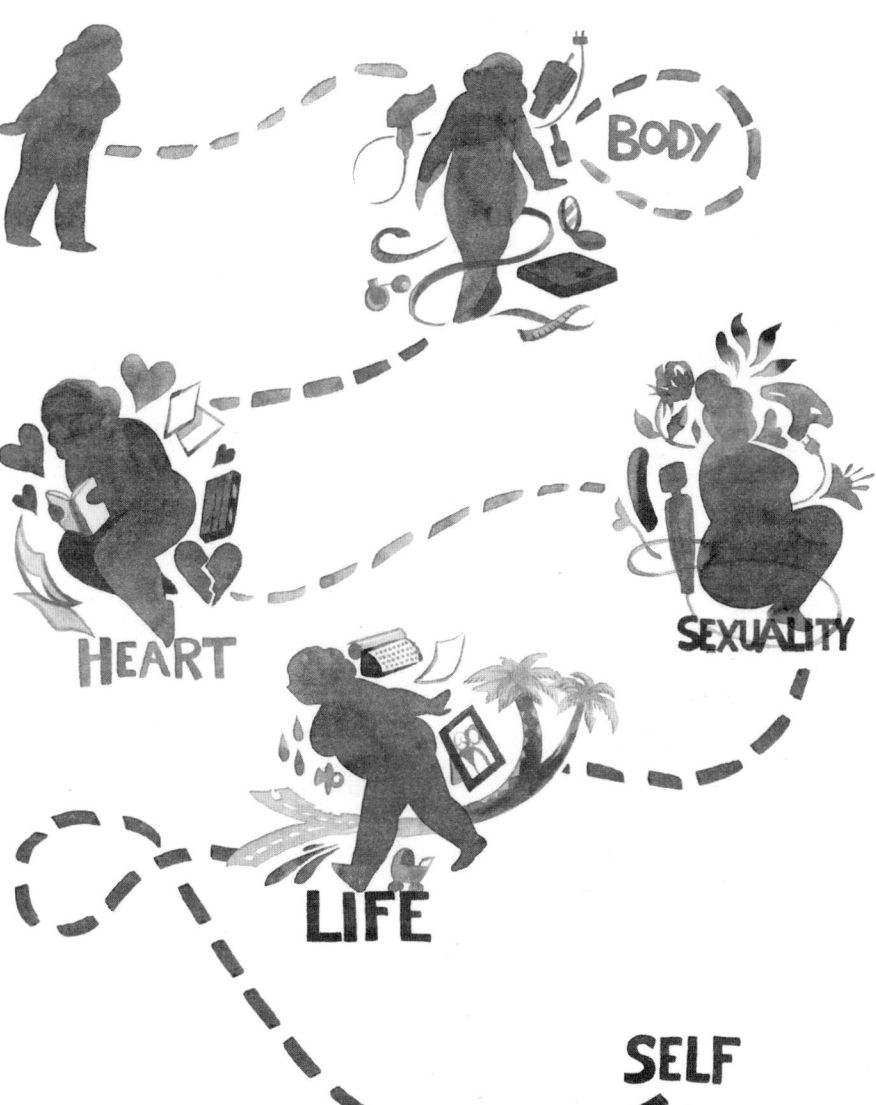

BODY

HEART

SEXUALITY

LIFE

SELF

LIFE

Things i know on the day i turn 30:

Nothing at all (and everything i need)
We're made for sun and grass and sugar and trees
If you're hollow and they say it's love – leave
Some people need you to be the problem – breathe
The You who is Forever is young and unafraid
You will lose her for years but She will stay
It is a heartbreaking miracle to feel all you do;
Write, paint, sing, cry, whenever you need to
Everyone is shit at driving sometimes and
Nobody has noticed that patch of sweat
The skincare stuff is trial and error and
For fuck sake when you're ill – rest
Sex isn't shorthand for connection
And being wanted won't make you whole.
Forgive yourself for believing both,
You were only ever doing as you were told
You are bigger than big and smaller than small
Emails get missed; you can't carry it all
You are surrounded by love, even when you're numb
Do another day; see what things become
You will not save or destroy with one plastic bag;
Moral perfection is a myth, we're all good and bad
The space in your brain belongs to you

THE SCRIPT

Line it with peace and comfort and your own truth
When the sun chooses you, stand in her warm
Speak to the ancestors and call your mum
You're allowed nice things but things is all they are
Meet their gaze when you walk in, you got yourself
    this far
Say thank you to strangers and Sundays and the sky
Bow to past pain so it can pass by
There is time to be held, to wander, to play
It's ok to not know, and do life anyway

THE PATH

We all know what is expected of us: we will work hard throughout our school years to secure our place in higher education. We will earn degrees that lead to steady careers, a savings account and a ladder to climb. We will meet a man and fall in love and decide to buy a house. We will settle down, have children, pick up a hobby and go on holiday once a year. We will retire and age quietly until it's all complete.

Even if we're never overtly told that this is the path we should take, the underlying blueprint is always there. It's reinforced by family expectations, cultural messaging and social comparison. There is an ever-present pressure to follow the expected route.

I fell off at the second hurdle.

I was always an academic overachiever, a straight-A perfectionist who stayed out of trouble and happily completed the group project all by herself. By the time university applications rolled around I had the grades to go anywhere I wanted. I also had debilitating anxiety and bouts of depression that knocked me out of life completely.

I didn't understand how I was supposed to decide where to go or what to study so I did what made sense to me at the time: chose the most impressive place, and the subject that I was the best at. I didn't know anything about the city I would move to or how I would survive by myself, but I was on the right path, the one that I was supposed to follow, and that was what mattered the most.

Three months after the course began, I sat in the passenger seat of my dad's car, the boot stuffed with my teenage belongings, fighting tears the whole way home. I couldn't do it. I'd failed. And the shame nearly ate me alive.

I'd tried to keep up with the workload and burned myself out into illness after illness. I'd tried to find my way around a big, unfamiliar city and had panic attacks in tube stations and on buses. I'd tried to be the best at every subject, but I was out of my depth and the pressure made my brain feel like it was exploding. I'd tried to find support and come away with nothing. I couldn't try any more.

We drove home in a tense quiet, both of us avoiding the question that would inevitably come next: what was I supposed to do now?

I never thought I'd be the one who fell off the path. It was meant to be plain-sailing for me – I had all the ingredients and all of the potential to hop from milestone to milestone without a blip. I should have been able to follow the expected route and end up fulfilled and happy, just like the blueprint says.

But the blueprint didn't fit the way it was supposed to – it doesn't for so many of us.

The blueprint doesn't accommodate people with brains that work a bit differently, or people whose strengths lie outside of academics. It doesn't acknowledge non-traditional career paths or the economic reality of adulthood today. The blueprint is hetero-normative and capitalist by design, assuming that all people fit the same boxes and want the same things. The blueprint is outdated and incomplete, but we're still struggling under the expectation that we'll make it fit.

In 2022, relationship support charity *Relate* conducted a survey which found that 77% of millennials and 83% of Gen Z are currently feeling pressure to reach life milestones like getting married, having children and buying a house.[23] Only 66% of over-seventy-five-year-olds reported feeling the same pressure when they were younger. Gen Z were the ones most likely to point out that they felt the pressure coming from social media.

Every time we scroll we witness the milestones of hundreds of different people. We know when someone we went to primary school with gets engaged and exactly how sparkly the ring is. We know when the person who used to do our hair has a baby and how perfect their growing family seems to be. We see endless updates from people we will never meet celebrating their six-figure businesses, life-changing travels, lavish wedding ceremonies, shiny cars and limitless designer outfits. We have never had more opportunity to compare ourselves to others than we do right now.

According to social comparison theory, humans are naturally driven to evaluate their own status by comparing themselves to other people. We work out how well we're doing in life by looking at others and judging how we measure up to them. Sometimes we engage in downward social comparison: comparing ourselves to people who are worse off than us and coming away feeling better about ourselves. But online, we're much more likely to compare ourselves upwardly, looking at people who we perceive to be doing better than us and using them as either motivation, or as proof of how far behind we are.

A hundred years ago, the number of people we had to compare ourselves to was dramatically smaller than it is now. We knew what was happening in our local community, and we might have picked up on the business of a handful more people via magazines and newspapers, but there was nowhere near as much opportunity to measure ourselves against others as there is now. In 2024, the average social media user spent two hours and twenty-three minutes online – that's hundreds, if not thousands of opportunities to compare.[24] And to make things worse, the majority of what we're comparing ourselves to isn't even real.

What we see online are carefully curated glimpses of whatever life someone wants to portray. We're usually only seeing the best bits: the most impressive achievements and smiliest, posed snapshots. We take other people's highlight reels and compare them to our behind-the-scenes, wondering why our lives are so mundane and monotonous when everyone else seems to be in a constant state of adventure, achievement and blissful happiness.

We see the magical, fairytale wedding, but we don't see the months of couple's counselling, the moments the relationship nearly ended, the financial strain of paying for it all or the family members arguing in the background.

We see the big, impressive job promotion but we don't see the stress headaches and sleepless nights, the sacrificed time with family and friends or the plates piled up in the kitchen sink.

We see a body that we think is perfect, but we don't see the disordered eating habits, the going to bed hungry, the list of tweakments and cosmetic surgeries, how the body looked before it was edited beyond what's humanly possible in real life.

Even if we have an understanding of how contrived the content we consume might be, the trap of comparison can still creep up and catch us. I've been a content creator for ten years and I still come away from scrolling with a sneaking sense of inferiority, like I'm just not measuring up. It's all too easy to believe what we see, and decide that we're in second place, not doing enough, falling behind.

The traditional life path doesn't only tell us what we're supposed to do, it tells us when we're supposed to do it. Too many of us are carrying around checklists of what we're meant to achieve by the time we turn twenty-five, or thirty, or fifty. If we don't meet our self-imposed deadlines, we take it as proof that we're failing at life, as if all of this is a race and we haven't finished in time.

When I dropped out of university, I was so sure that I was being left behind. I pictured everyone else rushing ahead, getting on with life, and there I was: small and scared with no idea what to do next. I was furious with myself and I couldn't believe that I had let myself fall so far from everyone's expectations, so far from the path.

It took years to see that version of myself in a more forgiving light. I wasn't a failure, I was a teenage girl with severe mental health issues who needed more support than she got. I wasn't falling behind, I was dealing with the hand I was dealt the best that I could, I just needed more time to be okay. I wasn't the problem; the pressure to follow a path that wasn't accessible to me was the problem.

I never did get back onto the expected route, and I don't think I was meant to. I know people who have followed the path perfectly and it's suited them just fine. Some people thrive knowing exactly where they're going and having a timeline to work towards. I also know people who've hit every mark on the timeline and don't understand why they still feel so unfulfilled. The traditional life path isn't good or bad, it's just one option of many equally valid ways to do life.

Maybe it fits us and maybe it doesn't, but we know better than to keep placing our value in arbitrary cultural standards that were never designed to accommodate us all. Why would we keep trying to force ourselves to fit the same old blueprint when we were always meant to be brilliantly, unpredictably, and beautifully our own.

CHILDREN

I am not the first thirty-something-year-old woman who does not know if she wants children.

There are plenty of us out here: the ones who are still waiting for certain parts of life to fall into place before they take the possibility seriously. The ones who feel like they're only just figuring out how to parent themselves, let alone someone else. The ones who can list off every reason for and against but seem to be missing a gut feeling either way.

I've been waiting for certainty to kick in for years – that magic click that people speak about when they just *know*.

I want to be able to conjure up a solid picture of what my life might become and be *sure* either way – *yes, I absolutely want to be a mother* or *no, I absolutely don't.* As of right now I can see myself going either way, both with equal (lack of) conviction.

There are lots of us who really aren't sure. In a 2019 YouGov poll, 28% of Brits aged 25–34 stated that they didn't want children at the moment, but they *may* want them some day.[25] Of those who said that they never want children, the top reasons why included the cost, the lifestyle impact of having kids, and believing that the world is already overpopulated. There are more factors going into the decision of whether to have kids than we ever thought there would be when we were pushing our baby dolls round the playground and imagining motherhood for ourselves.

We have more freedom than ever before to choose *not* to become mothers. It's a choice that has taken decades of convincing the world to see women as more than carriers of the next generation of men. We *have* a choice, and that can't be taken for granted.

For our grandmother's generation, the question wasn't *if*, it was *when*. *When will you have children? Not before marriage, of course. But not too long after. While you're still nice and young. And of course, you'll stay home while your husband works. Of course, you'll drop everything to be a full-time mum. Motherhood will be all you've ever wanted, of course!*

According to data from the Office for National Statistics, in 1971 only 18% of thirty-year-old women were child-free.[26] By 2022, that number had risen to 50%. More and more of us are opting out of having kids, and if we *are* becoming mothers, we're waiting until we're older than our mothers were.

There is an old VHS tape somewhere in my family home of my mother, rosy-cheeked and blue-eyed, being asked why she wanted to become a mum. When I first watched the tape I held my breath, waiting for something deeply sentimental that would help me reach some clarity of my own. My lovely mother, ever the practically minded, gives an answer about being good at organisation, and thinking that she would be well-suited to the task of raising children – not the moving response I was hoping for, but she wasn't wrong.

My mother's planning and organisational skills are unrivalled. She managed a household and the schedules of three children without so much as a forgotten permission slip. She was never late, never visibly overwhelmed, and a master at making limited funds stretch so that it was always enough. I remember watching her sail through the weekly food shop, gliding down the aisles to find the best offers and laying down coupon after coupon at the checkout. But even being as thrifty as she was probably wouldn't cut it in today's economy.

In 2024, the cost of raising a child from birth to age eighteen came in at £223,256, or £12,400 a year.[27] Meanwhile, the cost of buying a house has risen to 8.8 times the average person's annual salary (more than doubling since the 1970s), and 60% of millennials are in debt.[28] Even if we're sure that we *want* children, we're forced to reckon with the reality that we might not be able to afford them.

And whilst we're trying to make one of the biggest decisions of our lives, we have to navigate the cacophony of opinions from all around us.

If we choose not to have children there will be confusion and questioning. People will prod, trying to figure out *what's wrong with us, why wouldn't we want kids? Are we broken? Missing the biological chip that keeps our species alive?*

If we choose to have children, there will be a different line of questioning: *why would we want to give up our lives like that? Do we realise how hard it is? Are we equipped for the challenge? Have we fully considered our decision? Are we prepared to be the best possible parent?*

I remember a drama teacher from my teenage years who once sat the class in a circle and asked each of us what we wanted to be when we grew up. To nobody's surprise, I said that I wanted to act. The question moved round the circle, and we listened to everyone's life goals: to be a teacher, a surgeon, a rapper, an entrepreneur. It came to the turn of a quiet girl who excelled in every subject and spent her Sundays at church. She was the only one to say that her life goal was becoming a mum.

But like, what else do you want to be? The class jumped into questioning mode. *Just a mum*, she insisted. She wanted a husband and a house and kids, and to spend her time taking care of them all. Similar ambitions have been echoed online in recent years by a growing community of 'trad wives': women who advocate for a return to traditional gender roles, focusing their energy on child-rearing and home-making whilst deferring marital authority to their husbands.

The whispers followed the girl out of the classroom. We couldn't grasp how someone's only goal could be motherhood, even to our thirteen-year-old brains it seemed regressive; a waste of her potential to be a successful, independent woman. I still don't quite understand her decision now, but I have to recognise that the wins of the feminist movement have offered us choice, and just because her choice was different to mine doesn't necessarily make it the wrong one for her.

Interestingly, when people are chiming in on our choices, accusations of selfishness fly on both sides: we are selfish for not wanting children, for prioritising our own lives instead of giving ourselves to the noble job of child-rearing. We are selfish for having children, for prioritising our wants over the state of the world, which almost certainly doesn't need any more humans in it.

We are selfish and wrong either way, and there's no shortage of people willing to tell us so. Whilst making decisions about our own lives, women so often find themselves in a position where they can't seem to win.

* * *

One of my childhood friends recently had her first child. She's got the university education, ladder-climbing career, stable relationship with a reliable partner, and a mortgage on a house in the suburbs. When I asked her how she *knew* that motherhood was the right choice for her, she gave a slight shrug of her delicate shoulders, and said "It's the next step, isn't it? Something to do for the next twenty years."

The idea of spending the next twenty years being a mother before all else sends a chill down my spine, but it's possible that's just because of the version of motherhood that was modelled to me...

My mother parented on a superhuman level – she had the lunches packed and the kitchen cleaned before we woke up. She made herself available day or night to pick us up or drop us off. She planned, and prepared, and cleaned, and cooked, and shopped, and fixed, and nurtured like she was born to do it. Like she was always meant to be *Mum*.

And no doubt she learned to mother so fiercely in response to the needs of her children. There are three of us, and the eldest – my sister – was diagnosed with cerebral palsy at birth.

I'm not sure there's any way to prepare new parents for the reality that their child is disabled and will need round-the-clock care for the rest of her life. I know that so many people would crumble and never stop grieving. But my parents didn't waver. They adapted to accommodate my sister's every need, and fought tirelessly for her to have the full, happy, dignified life that she has.

While my dad worked to provide for the family, my mum handled most of the day-to-day care. She was equipped for every inaccessibility, every difficulty, every emergency. She strode forwards without complaint, my sister on her arm. *Mum* was her identity, first and foremost and always.

I remember her having a few small hobbies, but nothing much. I remember her having a few casual friendships, but not many. I remember her having one hour a week when she would go to the local pool and chat with the other mums while slowly swimming from one end to the other. Other than that hour, it was all motherhood, all the time.

I am so eternally thankful for the version of motherhood that she gave to us. And I am also so sure that I do not want it for myself.

The only version of motherhood that I would wish for myself – or anyone else – is one where we don't have to completely give up every other part of who we are, where we still have *some* time for ourselves and *some* sense of identity beyond mothering. I would still want my passions, my hobbies, my interests. I would want the Friday nights *and* the occasional afternoons. I would want to feel supported by a village in a way that I know she never did. I would want more, but I'm not sure if that's a realistic want.

There *are* people who parent differently – parents who don't follow gender roles, parents who take their children travelling, parents who raise kids in communities. The nuclear family that we default to today hasn't always been the norm, and still isn't across all cultures. Maybe I could be a different kind of parent... and I already know a hell of a lot about being a care-giver.

I started officially caring for my sister at nineteen – it was my own choice and it made sense for everyone involved. I'd dropped out of university, I had no plan, I love my sister and she was finally able to move into her own house and expand her care team beyond my parents. So, I moved in with her, part-time.

She lives in a lovely purple house with posters of pop stars from the 2000s on the walls and a never-ending supply of cola stacked up in her kitchen cupboard. Her disability means that while she is somewhat mobile, she will always need assistance with everyday life: cooking, cleaning, bathing, dressing, planning, getting around. All of the things that are quite similar to what a parent would do.

I know what it's like to be in charge of another person's welfare, to look out for their safety and protect them from potential dangers. I know what it's like to try to keep another human entertained, coming up with activities to fill their day and bring them joy. I know what it's like to do the practical stuff: the food planning and the bedtime rituals and the chauffeuring to social events. Even though it's not the same thing as having children, I have a pretty solid idea of how it might look to be a parent – probably more so than most people who don't have kids.

But even knowing what it's like to be a care-giver, I still find myself going round and round the reasons for and against becoming a mother, landing on the same *I don't know...*

* * *

When I started dating a woman, it dawned on me that the decision of whether to have kids wasn't going to be made by accident. There was no longer the possibility that a tipsy one-night stand or a missed birth control pill was going to lead to a moment of realising that *yes, I do want this. I do want to have a baby.* The first step to parenthood was going to have to be a very conscious choice, if I really wanted it.

I went to walk the dogs with my mum, yellowing leaves crunching under our feet. I asked her how she felt about the idea of grandchildren, knowing that I was the only remaining candidate for providing them. I expected her to say that she'd love some – I can see her so clearly relishing the opportunity to spoil and smother a baby with love and care while dispensing to me all of the hard-won wisdom that three kids had taught her.

"Well," she began immediately, like she'd had the answer pre-prepared, "I've done more than my share of caring already, and I think that there are other ways for us to put our goodness into the world than by bringing more people into it." She carried on walking, not breaking stride. I blinked hard to make sure I was actually conscious; it was such an un-Mum-like thing to say. But she wasn't wrong.

That *is* what I want more than anything: to know that I've put some goodness into the world. A child isn't a necessary component of that, but then again, raising the next generation to be compassionate, thoughtful, generous and accepting humans is an act of goodness in itself. Lord knows we need more parents who are healed enough to not pass their trauma down again.

It's only in the last couple of years that I've known any children. For most of my adult life there just weren't any around – my friends hadn't started building families and there were no younger cousins that lived close enough to babysit. I was completely unbothered about kids, leaning heavily towards not having any.

Then I met my girlfriend, with her giant, gorgeous family and parents who leave the door unlocked so that anyone can pop in for a cup of tea anytime.

"You're gonna love the girls," she said, talking about her young nieces, "they're so much fun." That afternoon they barged into the house with sparkly backpacks filled with toys and snacks and books. They looked at me, suspicious but intrigued: *a new person with bright pink hair... interesting.*

It only took a few visits for them to feel comfortable grabbing me by the hand and pulling me into whatever fantasy land they were playing in that day. I was given dolls and told the storyline. I was given pens and told where to colour in. I was reached up to with tiny, determined arms and told to lift, spin, carry, throw, use my grown-up strength to help them be fairies and super-heroes and witches.

By the end of the day, I was exhausted, bruised and not sure how to snap back into adult language. But my inner child was ecstatic. I realised that all the while I was playing, I wasn't worrying about anything else. I wasn't thinking about deadlines or household chores or whether I was doing enough. I was just there, present. Fully absorbed in the moment. I couldn't believe how much I loved it.

These have fast become my favourite days. I look forward to when we can visit again and I can spend some more time being the colourful, fun auntie. The parents get a break, and I get to soak up the hopefulness about the world that comes from being around young people who are so full of life. Maybe that's enough – maybe that's the role I'm meant to play. But then, on the other hand...

* * *

I think, at the moment, the only way to honour myself is to sit in the not knowing. Explore all of its corners and validate all of its concerns. I understand why the choice feels overwhelming. I understand the fear of getting it wrong. I understand why it's so difficult to tune out all of the outside noise and connect to our own knowing when it comes to this.

I might not be able to give myself an answer. But what I can do is witness this not knowing, listen to it, hold it gently, care for and nurture it, like any good parent would. And maybe, in its own time, the knowing will come.

FAME

I don't remember a time in my life when I wasn't in awe of celebrity.

Growing up, I read the gossip magazines, I watched the 'best dressed' segments of the Hollywood reporting shows, I lived for toxic reality TV. As soon as I was old enough to have pocket money, I spent it trying to dress like Paris Hilton, and I fantasised about how it might feel to one day be famous enough for masses of people to know my name.

Maybe I could be a singer... Or an actress! Or a model... I would be invited to all the most exclusive places... I would wear designer outfits on red carpets and have my picture taken by hollering photographers... I would be beautiful, and popular, and happy, like they all seemed to be. All I had to do was become a celebrity, and my life would be complete!

In my young mind, being famous was the ultimate achievement. If you were important enough for the world to know who you were, that meant you were special. Special in a way that set you apart from everybody else. Surely, there was nothing in life that could feel better than that?

During my teenage years, when I wasn't spending my spare time trying to make my body smaller, I was spending it keeping up with celebrity culture. I would go for long evening power walks with my best friend, both of us talking over and over what we'd eaten that day and the latest Kardashian drama we'd seen online.

We would make collages out of cut-up magazines, worshipping the thinness, style and allure that seemed to come with extreme fame. It was so far removed from where we were: living in a small, working-class town, hating ourselves, not knowing what would come next. The sparkle of Hollywood gave us an endless fantasy to escape to – a world where we could imagine being someone else. It was so enticing we could almost taste it, more delicious than any of the foods we no longer allowed ourselves to eat.

I broke away from that world when I found body positivity. Celebrity culture has always come hand in hand with diet culture: the impossible beauty standards that fame perpetuates, the hyper-focus on the bodies of celebrities, the obsession with what they eat and how they move and how we can look more like them. Fame, for women, has always been dripping in fatphobia and objectification, and for the first time, I didn't want that life for myself.

I stopped reading magazines with photoshopped stars on the front covers and articles about losing ten pounds in ten days. I stopped watching the TV shows that only ever showed one type of body as being worthy of love and excitement and adventure. I stopped keeping up with celebrity gossip – all of it was so appearance-focused and I was finally trying to find my worth beyond how I looked.

After I jumped off the diet cycle, I slowly accepted that I was never going to look like the Hollywood bombshell or the heroin-chic supermodel, and maybe I wasn't meant to. Maybe I wasn't made for that world. With a quiet sense of relief, I closed the page on my idolisation of celebrity culture and accepted that I probably wasn't meant to be famous, after all.

As I started to heal from the damage that diet culture had done – reconnecting to my body, reclaiming movement, learning to eat intuitively after so many years of restriction – I couldn't believe the sense of freedom that it brought. Finally, I didn't hate my body, and I was *living* again, instead of putting everything on hold until I'd made myself smaller.

I had to share this new way of being. I had to tell other women – women who were still stuck in the claws of diet culture – that there was another way to live! There was life beyond constantly striving for thinness! We have worth beyond how our bodies look! *Look! If I can break away, so can you!*

But then something unexpected happened: lots and lots of people started listening. The social media platform that I had previously been using to post pictures of dogs and fruit bowls was quickly filling up with thousands of people who wanted to hear what I had to say. Who wanted to see me and know what I was doing. Who saw me as important, in some way. And in not much time at all, in that small subsection of the internet, I became a bit... famous. And I had no idea how to handle it.

I kept doing what I was doing: sharing messages about accepting our bodies and being kinder to ourselves. I wanted as many people as possible to know that they didn't have to go through life at war with the way they looked. I carried on for years, not knowing what it might become or even if it would simply disappear one day.

But social media didn't disappear. It only got bigger and bigger until having a platform on it became a career in itself. Influencers were turning into the new micro-celebrities, and a whole different pathway was opening up in front of me. One that invited me into the periphery of the world I used to worship all those years ago...

I started being asked to go to shiny events with shiny outfits where photographers take shiny pictures. And of course, I wanted to see what it was like behind those doors! I started meeting more people who I used to look up to in magazines. Brands wanted me to promote things, to wear their clothes, to sit on a panel at a summit in New York.

It felt surreal. I waited for someone to tell me that they'd made a mistake and I wasn't meant to be there, but nobody did. So, I kept going, walking this new career path that teetered on the edge of celebrity, trying my best to hold onto my values as I went.

But underneath the shine and excitement, there was a kind of tension building that was impossible to ignore: all the toxic parts of celebrity culture are embedded in influencer-land, starting with the hyper-focus on appearance above all else.

Online, how you look is everything – being visually engaging gets you views, followers, opportunities and ultimately, can be the basis of an entire career. There are unrealistic beauty standards everywhere you scroll, enhanced by increasingly intelligent filters and editing apps. Our body parts are constantly turned into trends, from the shape of our eyebrows to the size of our waists, with influencers leading the way.

When I started going to more creator events, I quickly realised that most of them were just photo opportunities. A lot of people were spending thousands on hair and make-up artists, stylists and clothes only to get a good picture and then leave. They'd learned the celebrity formula: have the right image and be seen in the right places and your star will inevitably rise.

Even though it didn't align with my beliefs, I couldn't help but focus more on my own appearance, and whether I looked the part in these new, shiny spaces. I suddenly cared a huge amount about outfits, make-up, angles and poses. It is so hard to be in that world and not get sucked in.

At a lot of events, there was a hierarchy to navigate – sometimes it was unspoken, and sometimes people would bluntly ask how many followers you had before deciding whether to speak to you. So many interactions were transactional; if you couldn't get someone closer to their goal of being famous, they didn't want to know.

I watched my peers jump and squeal, barging through crowds to capture themselves breathing the same air as a very famous person so that they could cash in on their new social capital later online. Sometimes I felt myself getting caught up in the frenzy and reaching for my phone to do the same thing, even as a persistent voice in the back of my mind said *what are we doing? Why are we here? This isn't who we are or what we stand for...*

I did my best to balance the shiny side of things with more meaningful work. I rationalised that if I was going to be in influencer-land, then I could use the opportunities to still talk about the things that mattered – to take on important projects, fundraise, volunteer. There were plenty of people who used their platforms for good, I could be one of them!

But I felt like I was walking a tightrope, with fame-obsessed influencer culture on one side and my real values on the other, constantly checking to make sure I wasn't going to fall. At the same time, I didn't want to get off completely. Part of me still craved being there, in amongst the shine of it all...

Some years into my time in influencer-land, I was invited to the mecca of celebrity events. After spending an obscene amount of energy planning the way that I would look, I found myself in the epicentre of fame: flashing lights, extravagant décor, A-listers with entire teams following them around. I was seated at a table near the back, next to the other content creators who'd been deemed relevant enough to earn their place.

Most of us sat, glued to our phones, robotically documenting our presence at the event – we knew why we'd been invited and we knew we had to prove our value by posting promptly and effusively about how magical it all was.

I started talking to the woman sat next to me. She looked to be barely out of her teenage years and her dress was so restrictive she couldn't sit comfortably. I learned that she was a lifestyle and beauty influencer, with more followers than the population of some mid-sized countries. During the gaps in our conversation, she was frantically editing a video that a brand had demanded she re-shoot just a few hours before it was scheduled to go live. After this event she would go straight to the airport to shoot a campaign in Dubai, then to Paris for fashion week, then over to the US for a string of very important appearances. It seemed like she was crossing over from influencer-land to the realm of genuine celebrity.

Her eyes were vacant as she told me about the life that she no doubt once dreamed of. Our food arrived: tiny, aesthetic portions that we took photos of immediately. Her dinner went untouched. Later that evening, I tee-tered to the bathroom where she was on the phone to her management team, stifling tears of exhaustion as she expressed how badly she needed a break. I touched up my lipstick in an ornate gold mirror and went back to my place, looking around me for the happiness that we've all been told waits for us inside the shiny gates.

* * *

One thing that celebrity culture does brilliantly is convince us that fame is the route to ultimate fulfilment. Once we reach the VIP circle, surrounded by luxury, adored by millions, then everything will be perfect and wonderful and we'll never feel sad again!

While there's no denying the huge amount of priv-ilege (primarily financial) that comes with celebrity, we should know by now that fame is not the cure-all solution it appears to be. If it were, there would be no famous people with mental health issues, struggling with addiction, or becoming one of the ones who leave us too soon.

The reality is that fame clashes with so much of what humans need to be truly fulfilled. Humans need connection. We need to be able to build authentic bonds and feel like we're part of a community. When you reach the heights of celebrity you have to be on guard against the potential ulterior motives of every person you meet – you can't simply be yourself and trust that people have good intentions. Going through life guarded and sceptical of each connection is a recipe for loneliness, no matter how many people are flocking to be in your light.

Then there are the expectations. When the public have elevated someone to the realm of stardom, there's an entitlement embedded in the relationship. We expect our favourite celebrities to say the right things, to make the art we want them to make, to show up in ways that are pleasing to us and to divulge every detail of their lives. This entitlement feels justified because we got them there! We *made* them! And if they deviate from what we expect, they'll be reminded that we can break them, too.

We claim to love our celebrity idols, but all it takes is a minor transgression from our projected idea of who they should be and we're ready to drag them down from their pedestal. Too often, we don't allow celebrities the grace of being human – of making mistakes, miscommunicating, changing their minds. We demand a perfect representation of whoever we believe them to be, which might not be who they are at all.

We feel like we *know* celebrities, especially in the age of social media when it's easier than ever to build para-social relationships. In reality, we consume a public persona that's often co-ordinated by entire teams of people. Yes, there is a real human behind the layers of protection and performance, but we don't treat celebrities that way.

We have seen, time and time again, the treatment that famous *women* especially are expected to put up with without complaint. They are torn to pieces by the press – their bodies dissected, their words twisted, their personal lives interrogated. They are hounded and harassed by paparazzi. They become hot topics as if their existences are up for public debate. And if they dare to advocate for their right to privacy, boundaries or respectful treatment, we're quick to label them as ungrateful, difficult and spoilt – after all, they *chose* this life.

So many of us would *still* choose to be famous, even knowing how toxic that world can be, and there must be reasons besides the money. Fame appeals to our egos – the part inside of us that wants confirmation: *yes, we are special! Yes, we are adored! Yes, people know who we are!* Our ego self might be even hungrier for validation if we've grown up feeling unworthy, unloved or not enough.

I still notice my ego self pulling me towards the bright lights, even after all we've seen looking in from the outskirts. The ego self is hard to resist, but it's also dangerous to put her in the driving seat, because she will never be satisfied.

There is no such thing as 'famous enough', especially to somebody who is using fame to fill a void within themselves. There will always be more events to be seen at, more followers to acquire, more headlines to reach.

People spend their whole lives chasing their next invite or viral moment, striving to stay relevant and sacrificing their sanity in the process.

And when we see the results of how toxic celebrity culture can really be to those within it: the mental health crises, the prevalence of drug and alcohol addiction, the reports of unethical, traumatising treatment, we see them as unfortunate stories that happen to individuals, rather than recognising that the whole culture is rotten.

* * *

Celebrity culture isn't going anywhere, the Kardashian/ Jenner sisters have over 1.5 billion combined followers on Instagram alone, and 57% of young people in the US want to be influencers.[29] We are still fascinated by the lives of the rich and famous, and we still want a piece of the limelight ourselves.

But maybe we could build a healthier relationship with celebrity. Maybe we could see through the shine and understand that it's all a carefully crafted illusion: no famous individual is as perfect, infallible or endlessly happy as it seems they are.

When they step out onto red carpets looking like an air-brushed dream, a team of professionals has co-ordinated their whole appearance, from the tweakments before the event, to the angle their hair falls across their face and exactly how to pose in the outfit they can't sit down in.

When they're being interviewed on prime-time TV they've been trained in exactly how to respond to be as likeable as possible. They've left whatever is *actually* going on in their lives at home, and have showed up ready to perform the version of themselves that the public wants to see.

When they launch a new make-up line, become the face of a major fast fashion brand or post about the product they can't live without, they are leveraging our idolisation of celebrity culture to make more money (that they don't need) by selling more things (that the world doesn't need in it) that they probably don't even use themselves.

Maybe we could re-evaluate what makes someone worthy of fame. Rather than building false idols based on how well they fit beauty standards or how excessively lavish their lifestyle is, we could direct our attention towards people who are worthy of being role models: people who stand for something, use their talents for good, invest in making the world a better place.

Even then, we could still recognise that our idols are only human. We could appreciate their contributions without worshipping their every move. We could hold them accountable for bad behaviour without expecting perfection. We could stop comparing ourselves to what isn't real and see that the road to true fulfilment isn't necessarily paved with paparazzi.

I don't fantasise about being famous in the same way that I used to. I know that it's not all it seems to be. I've learned that it's better to focus on what feels meaningful and authentic, rather than whatever looks the shiniest from the outside.

It is hard to see through the illusion of fame, especially if we've grown up enthralled by the lights. But it is only an illusion. One more moving target we're taught to chase so that one day we'll be able to say that we're important, special, worthy and enough.

I say we decide that we're already all those things, no fame required. And stop putting our time, attention and value into places that make us feel so much smaller than we are.

THE PRODUCTIVITY TRAP

I wake up and immediately start thinking about the work I need to get done today.

I get out of bed, tidy the kitchen, start the dishwasher and the washing machine. I answer emails while I drink my coffee, glance at unopened messages from friends and tell myself I'll get to them later. I have two meetings to go to.

I put on a podcast while I get ready so it doesn't feel like wasted time. I scroll through social media on my way to the station. On the train, I work on my own content: editing videos, writing captions, finding the perfect photos to post with a meaningful message. I switch myself 'on' for the meetings and smash them. I record myself in between and post it to my stories, to feel like I'm still doing something.

When I get home, I think about what else I can create – write a newsletter? Plan a workshop? Think of new content concepts? I take the washing out of the machine and tidy my bedroom. I call my internet provider and book an appointment with the optician. I make a list of toiletries I'm running low on.

I spend two hours editing a video and another hour sharing it, replying to comments, tracking how well it's doing. Then I try to come up with the next thing. I get ready for a podcast recording with someone on LA time and psych myself up so that I can be great and maybe that will help me get to the next big thing. I research ways to fix my posture and compare myself to other people who do the same job I do.

I check in with my diary and whether I need to order my repeat prescription and work on my book proposal. It's 9pm and I haven't had dinner. I make something quick and easy and struggle to zone out of the day while my head is still bursting with all the other things I could be doing with this time. I try to relax, not really relaxing, endlessly scrolling to feel like I've squeezed every last moment out of the day doing *something*.

I haven't replied to my friends or done anything you could call self-care. But I've been productive. I've tick-tick-ticked my to-do list and pushed myself to make things and plan things and stay on top of my adult admin. I haven't wasted any time! Which means that on this day, I can feel okay. The guilt that hovers over my unproductive moments is quiet. All I need to do is wake up again tomorrow and do exactly the same – and the next day, and the next, and the day after that...

It creeps up on you, the need to *use* every minute of every day. The idea that if you don't, you're falling behind, being lazy, wasting your time. The idea that for your day to be worthwhile, you have to have something to show for it: a number of hours clocked in, money made, content produced, skills worked on.

When I was young and the school day ended, I couldn't wait to rush home and do absolutely nothing. The late afternoon hours would be filled with reruns of *Sabrina the Teenage Witch.* I'd lie on the carpet, twiddling my hair between my fingers. Maybe I would draw a bit, or play outside with the girl who lived across the road, or sing along to Atomic Kitten in my sister's bedroom. I went wherever my whims took me, not once worrying about whether those whims were productive.

Entire summers sprawled out with nothing to do but rest. No need to earn my place in the world by producing something of value for someone else. Only grass to skip through and limbs to move clumsily. Friends to maybe see and maybe not. No panic about wasted hours or what I might lose in the absence of productivity.

Adulthood comes around fast, and brings the unavoidable reality of navigating capitalism with it. Doing nothing turns into a rare treat to fit between all the responsibilities of being grown: working, paying bills, cleaning, maintaining relationships, keeping ourselves alive. Being unproductive has consequences for our livelihood, there's a layer of panic that comes with the idea of letting ourselves rest. Especially when it's becoming increasingly difficult to afford to be here, living.

But for a lot of us, our need to be productive has gone beyond necessity. We are not only working to the point of paying our bills, we're working to the point of exhausting ourselves. We've stopped playing. Stopped meandering. Stopped simply being. Our levels of productivity don't only define our success in one contained area of our lives, productivity is the new metric by which we measure our whole worth. And like a lot of other measures we've been given before, no amount ever seems to be enough. There's always another goal to reach. Another accolade to achieve. Another promise of praise or a pay-out.

I have friends who only feel good about themselves when they're grinding their way to guaranteed burnout. I know people who brag about making themselves sick from working too hard. There's a romanticisation of putting productivity above all else – above relationships, above wellness, above living.

A study by Mental Health UK titled the *Burnout Report* found that 91% of adults experienced high or extreme stress in 2024, and a YouGov poll revealed that one in five workers have taken time off for mental health issues caused by pressure or stress.[30]

When did life become this? When did we start holding ourselves to a standard that better fits machinery than human beings? Why are we so reluctant to give ourselves a break?

A lot of us are running on a scarcity mindset, believing that if we slow down, we'll be overtaken and somebody else will win what we've worked for. This isn't entirely imagined, it's how a lot of our jobs work, especially if we're freelancers. But the constant competition of who can have the least human needs in order to produce the most isn't sustainable. We're breaking ourselves.

In the past, when I have picked up the pieces of a friend's mental health after they've run headfirst into burnout, I've always told them the same thing: that if they never produced another thing, never made anything, never wrote anything, never progressed in their career or earned any more accolades, they would still have infinite value. They would still deserve to be here, existing peacefully, having their needs met, knowing that their worth isn't dependent on their productivity.

I try to tell myself this same truth, but the panic of not being enough stops it from being fully absorbed. *We have to earn this,* my brain says, *we have to keep being impressive and productive, otherwise why do we even deserve to be here?* This narrative of always having to earn something with my behaviour means that ironically, I can never fully enjoy whatever it is I've supposedly earned. There's always more to do, more to prove. And one day it will pay off. When? Who knows...

Once every few weeks I go to my sister's house and clock in for my shift as part of her care team. She wakes up in the mornings (whenever she pleases) and drinks a cup of tea. She checks in with the *Loose Women* and her other favourite morning TV hosts, giggling at their bad jokes and joining in with their debates. She logs onto her computer and starts dancing – some days she dances for hours to the songs we grew up lip syncing to in her bedroom.

We get dressed and go for a slow walk. We laugh at things that have all been said before, find ourselves some food and sink into the sofa. She goes back to dancing, singing, or flipping through a celebrity gossip magazine. Sporadically, she's consumed by writing. She types out hundreds of pages, one tap at a time, of the never-ending drama novel she's been pouring out for the last decade. She writes about things like hair salons and turbulent marriages and has no interest in ever showing the pages to anyone. She finds her way back to the sofa for the rest of the day.

I get her ready for bed, she sleeps, and the next day starts the same. My sister – who has cerebral palsy – will never be productive according to our current societal definition. She will never work, never make money for someone else. She will never manage her own home. She will never create things for other people's consumption. And she has infinite worth. She has worth simply because she is.

She reminds me that our obsession with productivity is not only rooted in capitalism, but ableism, too. There are many people who will never meet the criteria to be considered productive (including all of us at different stages of our lives – like when we're ill or injured or as we get older), and their right to exist does not depend on their output. Our right to exist shouldn't depend on what we produce.

What if we reframed productivity? What if we centred the idea that the most productive things are the things that lead to us being well, and whole, and human?

What if we saw it as productive to spend time with our family? Human beings need connection in order to survive, and a supportive community isn't waiting at the top of a career chain.

What if we saw it as productive to play? Adulthood is relentless and joy sustains us.

What if we saw it as productive to rest? Not necessarily so that we can bounce back and be more productive again afterwards, but because rest in itself is good for us. And how could things that are truly good for us ever be unproductive?

In recent years there's been a growing movement that frames rest as an act of political and spiritual resistance.

In *Rest Is Resistance: A Manifesto,* Tricia Hersey encourages us to disrupt the systems of capitalism and white supremacy by unapologetically claiming our right to rest. She reminds us that "We must believe we are worthy of rest. We don't have to earn it. It is our birthright. It is one of our most ancient and primal needs."

Imagine if we saw it as productive to pause and feel our feelings? Then we could move from a place of being healed rather than being hurt. Or if we prioritised being creative without the intention of commodifying whatever we make? How much happier would our souls be, expressing themselves without needing the results to be promoted or validated with purchase?

What if it was productive to just be? To sit somewhere and watch sycamore seeds spiral down to the ground. To notice the colours of the sky, smile on people who go past, focus on how the breeze feels. What if being present was productive?

Maybe it's not possible to entirely tap out of productivity in the time and place we live right now. But the least we can do for ourselves is not buy into the myth that we are only valuable at our most productive. We can refuse to flatten the meaning of our lives down to how much we can make for other people or how much we succeed, according to capitalist milestones.

Reducing our entirety to how much we produce is a prime example of making ourselves smaller, of erasing all that we are outside of one, limited way of measuring value. What about how we love and the connections we nurture? What about the things we enjoy and the way we express our inner worlds? What about the cultural rituals that have been passed down or the traditions we hold onto? What about all the things we are, when we're just *being,* instead of *doing?*

We are so much more than our productivity, and we deserve to start living like it.

GETTING LIFE WRONG

During the summer of 2021, I fell into a deep, dark depression hole.

The world had spent more than a year reeling from the fear and uncertainty of a global pandemic, and my brain had become a brutal place to be.

None of the ways I spent my time seemed to have meaning anymore; whether it was reading a book or talking to a friend, it all felt pointless, selfish and wrong. The things that used to feel good, like walking my dog or eating my favourite foods didn't feel like anything. I was just going through the motions while my internal narrative told me all the ways I wasn't enough on repeat.

I wasn't working enough, or helping enough, or being fun enough, or creative enough, or successful enough. I wasn't a good enough friend or sister or daughter. I wasn't making enough of a difference in the world. I was wasting my time and failing at being the person I was meant to become. I was getting life wrong.

Every night I told myself that I would wake up earlier and get things back on track. I would make better choices, get motivated, turn things around. But every morning my brain glitched awake and I was instantly overwhelmed by the thought of having to navigate my way through the day. So, I let the relief of sleep claw me back under.

When I finally woke up, the guilt of having overslept hovering over my head, I set about forcing myself to do the things I believed I *should* be doing. I dragged myself to my desk, staring hopelessly at emails I didn't know how to answer. I crawled out for a walk, coming back early because it felt like I was tugging my limbs through treacle. I would inevitably end up back in bed, giving in to the relentless chorus of self-hating thoughts that had hummed in my brain for months: I was awful, I wasn't enough, I wasn't equipped to do life, I was getting it all wrong.

The more airtime I gave the thoughts, the more embedded they became as my new personal narrative. Every day my self-worth fell lower, and I felt frozen: stuck in the same loop, unable to break out of the darkness.

Anyone who's fallen into a depression hole before will know that the only way to get back out is by taking small steps in the direction of *anything* that's good for you. Opening the curtains to let daylight in even though you don't want to. Having something to eat even when you've lost your appetite. Talking to another human, even though it feels impossibly hard.

I was lucky enough to have people around me who saw how far I had fallen, and who tried to show me the way when I couldn't see it myself.

I would call my dad in a panic and he would come over, take me out for a slow stroll or sit with me as I watched *Moana* for the sixty-seventh time, reassuring me that I was allowed to sink into a comfort film and rest. My best friend would cook us dinner and attempt to pull me out of my thought spirals by telling me all the details of her latest special interest: Korean pop music (I know more about BTS than I ever thought I would know).

They each encouraged me to lean into self-kindness, to give myself a break and seek out whatever felt fun. They tried to lure me into making future plans to look forward to, telling me that I could do whatever I wanted to do!

The problem was that I could barely see past the next hour, let alone into the future. And I had no fucking clue what I wanted, beyond being able to curl up into a ball and disappear. My depressed brain could barely decide which pair of socks to take from the drawer and wear. How was I meant to decide anything bigger than that? I would no doubt make the wrong decision, and make everything worse.

I've always been scared of getting life wrong. The fear that I could miss the path I'm meant to be on, make a decision that takes me in the wrong direction and end up somewhere I'm not supposed to be has followed me around for as long as I can remember. It shows up in patterns of obsessively overthinking every choice – even the small, mundane ones like where to eat or which vacuum cleaner to buy. I can spend three hours researching suction power and still not feel ready to commit.

The fear of getting life wrong separates me from being able to tell what I truly want. By default, a lot of my decisions have been based on whatever feels the least scary. I choose whatever has the lowest risk, or will bring the least judgement, or will make other people happy. And that's when I can bring myself to choose at all.

I'm all too familiar with decision paralysis: feeling stuck and unable to move in any direction because I just can't bring myself to decide. The safest option is to stay exactly where I am – not making any choice means I can't make the wrong one. But the longer you live like that, the smaller your life becomes. You stop being an active participant and become a passive character in your own story. If you're too scared to decide where to go, you go nowhere at all.

That summer, everything had built up around me to create the perfect storm. The pandemic had made the world feel scarier and more unpredictable than ever, every day was filled with doom-scrolling that disconnected me from all the good in my life. My anxiety went into overdrive, and depression joined the team, latching onto the narrative that no matter what I did, I was getting it wrong.

Each day I spiralled further down into the darkness, unable to see a way out, unable to make a move.

* * *

On a balmy afternoon in August, I sat in a doctors' waiting room, willing every muscle in my body to not run away. The people I trusted most in the world had all agreed: it was time to ask for more help.

I'd managed to make the call, even as my leg twitched and tears pricked at the corners of my eyes as soon as the dial tone started.

"What was the appointment regarding?" a kind-sounding woman asked.

"I think I need to talk to someone about my mental health," I managed, trying to sound as okay as possible. I immediately felt like a fraud – if I was well enough to make a phone call, then surely I wasn't sick enough to need this appointment?

I waited for my name to show up on the screen, noticing the pamphlets that decorated the walls warning people about the flu, heart disease, stroke. When my turn came, my legs were ready to dash out of the building, but instead they walked me into the doctor's office and sat me down, where I began to sweat all over a small plastic chair.

I had no idea how I would even begin to sum up what living in my brain felt like to a stranger who was no doubt over-worked and eager to get on to the next patient. I felt guilty, and stupid, and like I should have been able to figure this out by myself. I cried as soon as he asked me how I'd been feeling, and apologised before saying anything else.

I left with a prescription that I was scared to take. It felt like losing control, admitting defeat, like I was weak for needing chemical assistance to get myself out of this place when surely if I just tried harder, I could do it myself.

I worried that I would turn into a completely different person, that it would change me in ways I didn't recognise. But I had to admit to myself that I was stuck. And as scared as I was of getting life wrong, the way I'd been living couldn't possibly be getting life right.

The first couple of weeks and their side effects passed in slow motion. I dragged myself through chattering teeth and nightmares and sweating through sheets. I braced myself to not be me anymore. There was a strange sense of grief to it, of letting go of being so unwell. That version of myself wasn't happy in the slightest, but by that point she was familiar, and who would I become without her?

I waited for a new and unrecognisable me to show up, but she never did. All that happened was that my brain got slightly quieter. All of my thoughts seemed to slow down a bit, so that there was a gap between a thought entering and the downward spiral that had been so quick to follow. My fear response dulled – I wasn't jumping so much at loud noises or unexpected objects. It became subtly, ever so slightly, easier to exist inside my mind. Which gave me the space to start making some decisions.

They started small:

What would I like to eat today? Is there anything I might look forward to?

What would I like to wear? What colours or textures might spark a little bit of joy?

What TV show do I want to watch? Is there something that might hold my attention instead of just playing in the background while my thoughts take over?

I took the smallest steps forward, and entertained the idea that the things I was choosing were okay. They weren't wrong or bad. See? Nothing awful was happening!

The decisions started to get a little bit bigger.

Who do I want to spend time with this week?

Do I want to say yes to doing that job?

What could I do for myself that I would enjoy?

I started building up a bank of proof that I was capable of making decisions, doing things and being okay. Slowly, I was providing my brain with a new narrative: that I deserved to be alright, and that I was doing life just fine.

One afternoon, as the summer was slipping away and only the most determined holiday-makers remained, I went for a walk along the beach in my sleepy hometown. I could finally spend time alone in my brain without the barrage of everything that was wrong playing on repeat. I watched the families building sandcastles, the dogs chasing sticks into the sea.

The sun was setting in a hazy ombre of blues and pinks, and the water was so still she looked like she was holding her own breath. The salt air of my childhood felt healing inside my lungs, and as I breathed it in, a thought formed itself in my mind: a want. An idea of something I wanted to do simply because it seemed fun.

A frill of panic ruffled up my body, but before I could stop myself, I started. I pulled off my clothes until I was standing in my underwear, staring at the sea. The last of the heat painted me gold, and I stepped out into the water, feeling the soft sand between my toes.

I didn't care if I was being watched. I'd watched all summer as people ran and played for no other reason than to feel joy, and I'd denied myself that for so many months now. As I waded deeper into the water, I realised that this was one of the first spontaneous things I'd done for myself for a very long while.

I sank my shoulders under the cold and let myself float along the surface. The colours in the sky were swimming and so was I. I was allowed this. It felt good. I was allowed to feel good.

I walked home, drying off in the wind and decided to not tell anyone about my afternoon dip. It was for me – I didn't need anybody else to know about it or validate that it was an okay thing to do. I'd made a decision based on what I wanted and nothing bad had happened. What a powerful piece of proof to give my brain.

I kept adding to my bank of proof until the old narrative about getting everything wrong started to fade. Some days the familiar pathway still tried to light up, blocking my ability to see clearly and sending me back into spirals of panic. But I got up the next day and tried again. Tried to treat myself kindly, to trust my ability to make decisions, to believe that just maybe, I was enough.

Slowly – with every decision I made and noticed that the world didn't crash down afterwards – the panic started to get smaller. Answers came easier. Tapping into what I actually wanted felt possible again. And I started to feel more and more like the Megan I remembered being years ago. I started to feel more like an active participant in my own life, someone who could make plans and be present and enjoy things. Like my life had been given back to me.

When I had been frozen in depression and so sure that whatever I did was going to be wrong, a friend said something to me that my brain rejected at the time. She told me that there were no right or wrong decisions. There are only decisions, and then life adapts around whatever we choose. She reminded me of all the life decisions I'd made before, and all the ways I'd evolved along with them, leading me right here to where I am – still breathing. Still surviving. Objectively okay, even if it didn't always feel like I was.

The more I started to step back into my own life, the more I considered that maybe she was right. Maybe I didn't have to obsessively overthink every decision, endlessly weighing up the pros and cons until I was stuck in decision paralysis. People casually make decisions all the time and they survive. Even if it ends up not being the best choice, sometimes it leads somewhere more interesting than the best choice would have. People choose things and then change their minds, and their lives do not suddenly collapse into nothingness.

Maybe there's no such thing as a 'wrong' decision at all. Maybe we just decide, and then adapt.

Maybe I don't have to be scared of getting it all wrong because I'm capable of withstanding change and listening to myself for the next right move, whatever I choose.

Maybe I don't have to live in fear of getting life wrong.

* * *

Around six months had passed since I'd started trying to rebuild myself, and I felt like a new and improved version of me. I had decided to move out of my hometown and challenge myself to live in a big city. I had even decided to get a tattoo – something I never believed that I would be able to do.

The idea of getting a tattoo – of committing to something that will be on my body for as long as I exist – terrified me. I couldn't stand the thought that one day I would look down and regret my choice. That it would be a bad decision. That I would have gotten it wrong.

But one day, my brain lit up with the suggestion that maybe I'd quite like to get a tattoo. It was something new that I hadn't experienced before. And I had an idea for a design that would always feel meaningful to me.

I did some research and found an artist whose style I immediately fell in love with; her portfolio was filled with flowers and portraits in delicate lines and vivid colours. Her schedule was fully booked for the next year, but I decided to reach out anyway, just in case there was anything sooner. She replied to say that she'd had a cancellation the next week, and my brain said 'go'.

I drove across the country by myself (something I would have been too scared to do before) and got my first tattoo: a watercolour landscape of the fields where I grew up and walked my dogs every day, with flowers blooming to one side, the sun setting in the background, and a shadowed silhouette of my dog Topsy, my best friend, who passed away a year or so before, running up the path towards me.

When the artist had finished, my eyes swam with tears. Not only because the piece itself was so beautiful, but because I knew how many internal mountains I'd moved to be standing there.

And that feeling? The feeling of having listened to myself, of saying what I wanted out loud, and of trusting myself to make a decision? I couldn't believe how good it felt.

It felt better than every overly calculated choice. It felt better than going nowhere because it's safer. It felt better than basing my decisions on what would be best for everyone else. It felt scarier. But so much better.

BODY

HEART

SEXUALITY

LIFE

SELF

SELF

the Sun is for you,
too

even if
even if
even if

She knows
all You are
and She
chooses
Your skin
to tickle
with tomorrows

accept Her
touch
She makes
no mistakes

IDENTITY

"When I was young," the woman next to me lamented, "people described themselves by saying which bands they liked or where they grew up." She stood to signify the ending of our lovely middle-class brunch meeting. "Now my children list their sexuality, gender, race, size, all of it in the first line of their bio!" She looked at me for reassurance of the absurdity of it all. The woman was thin, white, wealthy, non-disabled and married to a man.

There will be people who read that last sentence and think "How is that relevant?", and there will be people who read it and think "Well, that tells us everything we need to know!" Regardless of where you sit, the woman was right about one thing: times have changed. Our understanding of identity has changed. The way we see ourselves and each other has changed.

I started thinking about my own identity at a young age. I grew up in a predominantly white, working-class town, with a Black dad and a white mum. Nothing felt out of the ordinary about this, until I noticed that I was the only one with brown skin in a classroom full of four-year-olds.

Somewhere between choosing the correct shade crayon for self-portraits and other kids holding up their arms to compare their colour to mine, I became increasingly conscious that I was different. I arrived home one afternoon to my mum asking the usual questions about how my day was, and famously said to her "I don't know anything! I don't even know if I'm Black or white!"

She chuckles whenever she takes that one out of the memory box, dusts it off and recounts it to someone new. At the time she told me, simply, that I was both. And ever since then I've been deeply aware that I am both, and neither, and somewhere in between.

My race was the first part of my identity that I tried to pin down, one way or the other, and ended up landing inescapably in the middle. Since then, it's become a familiar feeling.

There have been years of questioning my sexuality, feeling not-straight-but-not-queer-enough.

There have been years of trying to work out where I fit within the world of body positivity, being not-quite-thin and not-quite-fat and navigating thousands of opinions on what that means I should say and do.

And while there are undeniable privileges to being in the middle of things, there's also a whole lot of questioning, and not quite understanding where you fit. Humans love absolutes. We crave clear answers and fall into a dichotomy all the time. It's this or that. Good or bad. Black or white. Grey area is uncomfortable for us.

For a long while, I wanted to just be one thing or the other, so that I could fit myself more neatly into the boxes I'd been presented with, and understand who I was supposed to be. Especially as I got older and identity politics became my lens for understanding the whole world.

My dad was the first person to teach me about social justice, always emphasising how important it was to treat people with respect, regardless of our differences. I learned about racism young, from his stories and from my own experiences, and I grew up with a disabled sister, so I saw ableism every day.

But outside of my family, I didn't have much of a chance to learn about different identities. I was quite far into my life before I knew anyone who was openly queer. Because of where I grew up, I didn't have any friends who weren't white until I was a teenager. And even with a disabled sibling, I didn't understand the politics behind disability rights. It wasn't until I started actively following a diverse range of voices on social media that I realised how expansive – and important – identity could be.

When I entered the world of body positivity, I followed fat activists who spoke about fat liberation and how body politics are all connected. From there I found anti-racism advocates who taught me about critical race theory. I learned about disability rights from disabled creators, and about the fight for trans equality from trans activists.

Identity politics felt like the missing piece of the puzzle to explaining why the world is the way that it is. Everything made more sense once I could clearly see the hierarchies that society has created to uphold power for some groups, whilst taking it away from others.

Before long, I was completely absorbed in the online social justice movement, thinking about identity politics all day, every day. I was hyper-aware of the identities of people all around me, and I looked out for injustice everywhere I went. On the plus side, I was more socially and politically conscious than I'd ever been, but on the other, I was engaged in a way that at times, started to feel obsessive.

Whilst I was striving to be a perfect social justice advocate, I was also endlessly questioning my own identity, and where I fit within the movement.

My brain was filled with the opinions of thousands of people I'd never met telling me what it means to be Black, to be white, to be a woman, to be queer, to be marginalised. So much of what I was absorbing was presented as an absolute – no nuance, no exceptions.

I was being told that Black people all experience one thing, and white people all experience another – so where did my experience sit?

If queer people are allowed to take up space, but I don't feel queer enough to claim it, where do I go?

If fat people should be listened to about body politics, and thin people should be quiet, should I speak?

I spiralled round and round, debating all these parts of myself that I'd always been unsure of and coming up more confused than ever. In amongst the noise there were plenty of people ready to tell me what I should call myself, what I should believe, how I should speak and who I should be. Unfortunately, they never seemed to be able to agree on a clear-cut box, either.

* * *

One afternoon during those hazy pandemic days, I went for my usual walk. I'd spent the morning waist-deep in social media comment sections declaring the right and wrong things for people to do and say depending on their level of privilege.

As the grass brushed past my ankles, I practised my contortionism: trying to fit my individual life experience into the boxes put in front of me.

It was a couple of months after the internet had exploded with protest signs and capitalised infographics about white supremacy following the murder of George Floyd by the US police force. The grief and justified rage rippling through the Black community was palpable. White people everywhere who considered themselves to be allies were reckoning with their own privilege and place in upholding racialised systems. And the mixed-race people of Black and white heritage who I knew were doing both, *feeling* both.

I had grappled with this part of my identity for as long as I could remember, but this was the most urgent it had ever felt. I *had* to figure it out: what was I, *really?* How should I be describing myself? Which community did I belong to? And what is my role in dismantling this system?

I found myself interrogating every racialised experience I could remember.

I remembered the first time I was called a racial slur at school – the other kids weren't sure how to label my ambiguously brown skin, so I heard the full variety over the years. I remembered the countless times I've been fetishised for my skin colour, called exotic and painted as some kind of stereotype. I remembered the people my mum would stop and speak to in the street, correcting them when they assumed that my white friend was her daughter. I remember all of the racist jokes that were thrown around in front of me, justified by saying that they're not really about me because I'm only half.

But then I counter those memories with the knowledge that my proximity to whiteness has afforded me so many privileges. I know that I have been granted more access because of my lightness. I know that I have been seen as more desirable because beauty standards are inherently racist. I know that I haven't experienced serious violence because of the colour of my skin, unlike my darker skinned friends. And I know that often, people don't see me as Black at all. I am *something*, not completely white but pale enough to avoid the worst kinds of prejudice.

So, what does that make me? I've always referred to myself as 'mixed-race', but it often hasn't felt like it's told the whole story.

I called my dad, the man who is so practised at holding my jumbled anxieties and helping me make some sort of sense of them. I told him that I just couldn't seem to figure this one out. All these years after I first came home from school and asked that simple question, I still didn't know the answer. *Am I Black or am I white?*

My dad answers that I am one hundred percent, completely, both. And that I do not have to see myself as two halves of a thing when I am a whole.

Being biracial is undeniable proof that two things can be true at once. Those of us with Black and white ancestry can experience anti-Black racism whilst also benefitting from colourism depending on the shade of our skin. We can assimilate into multiple different communities whilst simultaneously not feeling a full sense of belonging anywhere. We will be seen as both too much and not enough depending on the context we're in. We can be privileged and marginalised at the same time.

And no two mixed or biracial people's experience will ever be exactly the same.

It isn't a question of this or that, black or white, it's a whole lot of grey area that we have to get comfortable being able to hold, otherwise we'll always be tearing ourselves in two.

After the urgency of that time settled down, I decided that I wanted to learn more about my family history and delve deeper into my heritage. I dug out old photos, talked to relatives, and read everything I could find, including a book called *The Jippi-Jappa Hat Merchant and His Family* that details generations of my ancestors on the Jamaican side, and their lives as one of the earliest families to emigrate to the UK.

My grandmother, Pauline Henriquez, was the first Black actress to appear on British television. After her acting career, she spent decades dedicated to social work, advocating for the rights and well-being of young, unmarried mothers, and was awarded an OBE in 1960. I remember her as Granny Paul, the one who read me stories about sugarplum fairies and sat on the grass while I tried to do cartwheels all afternoon. She was the epitome of Black brilliance, and I am proud to carry her in my genes.

Sometimes, when a camera catches me at a certain angle, I look a little bit like her. And sometimes, on a different day, I look a little like my mum, whose ancestors have lived in England as far back as we can see, and who is the most patient, dependable and resilient woman I've ever known. My face carries both sides, exactly as it was meant to.

After years of questioning, not knowing what to call myself and not being sure of where I fit, I know one thing for certain. I am exactly as I am meant to be: both, and neither, and somewhere in between.

* * *

Culturally, we are more aware of identity than we have ever been. We have to be, if we want to build societies where people who have been marginalised because of their identities are fully seen, and respected for every part of who they are.

There is power in claiming our identity. It can lead us to community, connection and to understanding ourselves and the world better. But when we're having conversations about identity politics, we need to hold onto nuance. The boxes that we've been given aren't one-size-fits-all. As important as it is to understand the characteristics that make people who they are, we also have to remember that no person can be reduced to those characteristics alone.

Every one of us is more than the boxes we fit into or the labels that are placed on us. And we are each entitled to go about the business of living – collecting experiences, honing our values, leaning into the things we love – and building nuanced identities that can't be fully captured by a list of nouns alone.

Figuring out our identity, for some of us, is a lifelong process. We might change over time, discover new things, refer to ourselves in different ways. And all of it's okay. Wherever we land, however long it takes, I hope we always know that we are each exactly as we're supposed to be. I hope we embrace ourselves in our fullness, whatever our identity.

GOOD PERSONHOOD

For a lot of years, birthdays meant baking.

When my dad's birthday came around, I'd make little round pastries filled with currants and raisins. For my best friend: a savoury pie with spinach and feta. And on my brother's big day, it was time for the annual triple chocolate salted cookie dough squares (yes, they taste as good as they sound).

Whenever the occasion called for it, I was ready to dust a kitchen counter with flour and spend my afternoon weighing and mixing so that I could bring something filled with love to a person who I love. It would usually go along with a sentimental gift that I'd spent hours making or finding. I took a lot of pride in doing birthdays well. It was part of what I believed made me a Good sister, a Good daughter, a Good friend.

Being Good meant practising thoughtfulness, generosity and compassion. It meant showing up and listening, remembering the important stuff and staying fiercely loyal. For a long while, being Good to the people in my life was a core component of what I believed Good personhood was all about. And Goodness has always been the goal.

My parents taught me the importance of being a Good person, and they each modelled it in their own way. Dad was always standing up for what was right, calling out injustice and advocating for other people. Mum was the first to offer time that she didn't have to help just about anyone with anything. Alongside their influence, there was the inescapable narrative of what made a Good Girl: obedience, politeness and friendliness at all times. In amongst it all, I grew up as the ultimate goody-two-shoes who had zero personal boundaries and *always* did the right thing.

I followed rules and respected people in positions of authority. I shared whatever I had with anyone who needed it. I was the first to offer help with anything and the last to complain. I did every piece of homework on time and I never had a detention.

I nailed Good personhood as a child. In fact, I really could've afforded to be a bit less Good – talked back to a teacher now and again or kept playing instead of leaving the game early to do more school work. But I had a clear code, and it helped me make sense of life.

When you're young, the parameters of Good personhood are much more contained. You don't have the pressure of difficult adult decisions, like figuring out how you're going to make a living. Instead, you have clear rules about which behaviours are acceptable and which aren't: don't lie, don't steal, be kind and do as you're told.

As life goes on, the rules get less clear. Good and Bad don't feel as straightforward or binary. The older you get, the more complicated being a Good person becomes.

I started having major meltdowns about whether I was a Good person around the time I turned sixteen. I was just coming out the other side of two years of serious mental illness – the kind that makes you feel like a black hole swallowing everything good around you.

I'd lost most of my friends, had to leave school, and was trying to rebuild my character from scratch (I'd just been 'girl with anorexia' for a long time). It broke into my brain, on a short trip away with my dad, that maybe I wasn't a Good person at all. Maybe I didn't care enough about other people, or do enough for the world. Maybe I'd lost track of my moral compass. Maybe I was Bad.

I sank down onto the hardwood floor of the house we were staying in, and sobbed.

My dad waited patiently while I found enough of a voice to explain the anxieties swirling in my head before handling my moral crisis with the firm knowing he always had.

There was plenty of time to figure out what kind of person I was going to be, he explained. There was time to be a Good sister, a Good daughter, a Good friend. It was perfectly alright to not know exactly what being Good looked like right now – a lot of grown adults still didn't know. I was allowed to not know, and keep living anyway.

So that's what I did.

I tried out different versions of Good personhood as I went along: being the vegetarian who always has reusable bags ready for the supermarket. Being the doting girlfriend who continues to pick up dirty pants from the floor without complaint. Being the person who will always stop to listen to a stranger in need, and not even feel mad when she definitely gets scammed out of a significant amount of money.

Even though I always did my best to be Good according to whichever guidelines I was following, there was a constant nagging feeling that I could be *better*. I could be doing more, trying harder, reaching a new level of Goodness.

And then came social media, which would change my idea of what it meant to be Good, forever.

In the beginning, there were only grainy selfies and pet videos; online activism hadn't found its place yet, so the amount of self-reflection after your average scroll was minimal. But it wasn't long before every social cause had its own space, its own hashtags, and its own advocates.

Over the years, my online world filled up with more and more people who were encouraging others to be Good, according to the values of their cause. I soaked up every single one, hungrily trying to turn myself into someone Good enough.

I followed people who taught me how many everyday phrases are Bad, and how many businesses are evil. They taught me that it's Bad to enjoy problematic films and TV shows, even if they used to be your favourite. It's Bad to be apolitical and turn away from any injustice happening in the world. It's Bad to be unaware of your privilege in any situation you go into. The last thing I ever wanted to be was Bad, so I absorbed these new rules into my daily life, and kept searching for more ways to be better.

I found people to tell me which supermarkets are ethically Good and which song lyrics are misogynistically Bad. People to teach me how Bad it is to support fast fashion and how Good it is to no longer travel by plane. People to prompt me to find new ways of being a Good ally to each marginalised group every single day. I was starting to see how I could finally be a person who was Good enough, *I just had to get it all right.*

And amongst the never-ending directives on how to be Good, were the stars. The shining examples of humans who seemed to be so Good you wondered how they could even exist. Individuals who were leading protests, changing legislation, travelling everywhere by an electronically propelled boat. *They* seemed to be able to do it all perfectly, never making a single unethical move. If they could do it, why couldn't you?

I've always had the tendency to do things by extremes, and trying to turn myself into a flawless example of Good personhood was no different. Very quickly, my parameters for what was Good enough exploded from being Good to the people in my own life to helping save the entire world. And there was no room to slip up.

I saw it as my personal responsibility to take on the rules from every cause, and practise them faultlessly. The way I spoke changed. The way I ate changed. The way I shopped changed. I stopped reading books for fun and started reading whatever the internet declared to be a Good person learning resource at that time. I threw out my old problematic faves and carefully monitored my response to anything that was meant to be funny or enjoyable.

Over time, I began talking myself out of going places or making plans because they would all involve something that wasn't Good. I spent hours deliberating over simple decisions because there were always Bad things to factor in. The more Good I told myself I had to be, the smaller life got, and the guiltier I felt.

The guilt started to swallow everything. An unnecessary piece of plastic packaging could sink my soul. A suggestion in my comment section that I hadn't talked about the latest world tragedy enough would break me. The inescapable reality of needing to make money to buy things like food and pay my bills felt so shameful that talking about any kind of work seemed like admitting to a horrible crime.

I was completely consumed by this new, impossible standard of Good personhood, and no matter how hard I tried, it never felt like I was being Good enough.

* * *

In the 2016 sitcom *The Good Place,* a group of people find themselves in the afterlife, grappling with the life decisions that landed them there. Some of them are self-proclaimed shitty people. Some of them are seemingly shining examples of Good personhood, having spent their lives helping others, raising money for charity or teaching spiritual enlightenment.

After trying to figure out how they all ended up in the same place, they come to realise that the scoring system for whether a human has been Good enough during their lifetime is a mess. Tiny decisions like which avocado to buy for lunch are scored based on the web of environmental factors attached to avocado farming, which the avocado buyer is oblivious to. A person can score +4.98

moral points for hugging a sad friend, but then lose 53.83 points for accidentally disturbing a coral reef with their flipper. Every single action is calculated way beyond the understanding or intention of the individual.

They also learn that the threshold for true Good person-hood is through the roof, and only a handful of people make the cut each decade. The show nailed the impossibility of being fully Good in this current time and place we live in.

We're more aware than ever of the Bad that exists all around us. We take in more tragedies from across the globe before we've had breakfast than our ancestors used to absorb in a lifetime. We're also painfully aware of our own part in the Bad, how our individual choices are add-ing up to create the world we live in. We are constantly learning new ways that the things we do are unethical, harmful, not Good. Like there's a moral minefield behind every decision and none of us were given a map.

Trying to figure it out almost feels like a set-up. As if we missed the memo at birth that said "Welcome to Earth. Nearly anything you choose to do with your life will contribute to the harm of someone else or the planet in some way. Enjoy!"

This is how late-stage capitalism works: the Bad is woven into so many layers of our everyday life that it feels impossi-ble to untangle things and extract what's Good from what's Bad. A lot of big Bad corporations also work very hard to convince us, the individuals, that it's entirely our responsi-bility to change all of our habits, and that will be enough to fix everything. In reality, it's global industries that should be taking the majority of the responsibility, since they are the ones with the power to make the most impactful change.

Yes, our choices can still make a difference, but a lot of us are swimming in guilt every time we fail to be morally and ethically perfect within a system that's designed to make Good choices the least accessible option.

If we want to sustain being Good, whilst also staying sane, we need to find the balance between caring about people, the planet and the impact we're having, whilst still living our lives, and not feeling completely shit about ourselves with every choice we make.

* * *

A few years ago, whilst I was at the height of my moral perfectionism, I went to meet a friend for coffee. They were an advocate for all things social justice, using their online platform to encourage people to engage with social issues and make Good choices – I looked to them when I was weighing up a lot of my own ethical decisions.

It was a grey winter afternoon, so I wrapped up warm and made my way across town to the small, independent coffee shop where we were going. I'd researched the place, so I knew it sourced its products sustainably and treated its workers fairly. I met my friend outside the train station and we hurried towards our hot drinks and a cosy place to catch up.

We got there, only to find that it was closed. And as we looked to each other to discuss our next option, the heavens opened and icy rain hailed down around us.

"Fuck it," my friend blurted out, as she hastily directed us back down the road and through the doors of the chain coffee shop that we both knew was a Bad place to be.

"Desperate times..." she said, shaking the sleet from her hair. I couldn't believe that she'd made such an imperfect choice, or that she'd been so casual about it.

As time went on, I started to meet more advocates in person who turned out to be not vegan, not donating all their spare time to charities, not living plastic-free, not always steering away from ableist language, not passing every professional opportunity to someone more marginalised than them. In short, they were not morally perfect. They were humans who cared about being Good, but who accepted that they weren't getting it right every single time. And they weren't holding themselves to the impossible standards that I'd absorbed for myself.

Moral perfectionism – just like all the other kinds of perfectionism – is unsustainable. It isn't realistic or even possible to be one hundred percent Good all the time. In real life, things are complicated, and being a Good person isn't an all-or-nothing equation. We each have our own challenges, responsibilities and limitations that factor into how much energy we can give to striving to be Good.

One person's version of Good personhood might look like trying to change the world, but for another, it might just look like trying to show up positively in *their own* world. Do one act of kindness a day. Or just get through the day making the best choices they can.

Maybe Good personhood is defined by trying our best to be Good, whilst understanding our own personal limitations and also *not sacrificing our sanity.*

When I was striving to be morally perfect, no Good thing I ever did felt Good enough. It didn't matter how eco-friendly my average day was. It didn't matter how much money I'd donated to Good causes. It didn't matter how many people personally told me that I had done something Good *for them*. I still went to bed with an overwhelming feeling that I was doing more Bad than Good, simply by existing. And that's no way to live.

Something I realised recently is that when my definition of Good personhood exploded to include trying to save the whole world, being Good in the ways that I used to believe in didn't feel like they mattered as much anymore.

I wasn't as bothered about birthdays as I was about spreading the word on the evils of giant corporations. I stopped being as sturdy a support system for my friends because I was so absorbed in things that were happening on the other side of the world. I didn't have anywhere near as much capacity to show up for my family because I'd already spent so much energy trying to post exactly the right thing about every cause on the internet.

Whilst I was busy trying to reach far beyond my sphere of influence, I was neglecting all the places closer to home. We each only have a limited amount of energy to give to things every day, and mine was constantly moving further away from the people around me, and the old ways I used to define being Good.

It clicked for me one weekend when I was scheduled to be with my sister. She has a rota of people to help with her full-time care needs and I was always on weekends. I'd spent the week in my usual never-ending rabbit hole of everything that was wrong with the world and all the ways we, the individuals, needed to do better. I packed my bag to head over to my sister's, got in the car (feeling awful that I was still driving petrol) and made my way.

As soon as I got there, I realised that I had nothing to give. I stood in her purple kitchen, waiting for the kettle to boil, aware that I didn't have a drop of positive energy to offer. My head was filled with unsolvable problems that I'd spent all week telling myself were my responsibility to fix. I felt exhausted, irritated and depressed – and it showed.

I got through the weekend doing the bare minimum whilst my mind was elsewhere. Everyone was okay, but nobody had a particularly good time. On the last evening before I went home, I was helping my sister through the usual nighttime routine: teeth brushed, face washed, pyjamas on, and from where she sat in the bathroom she looked up and said, "You're a Good sister, Megan."

The surprise hit me first, and then the guilt. I knew that I hadn't really been a Good sister lately, not in the way I'd always wanted to be. I wanted to be the fun and energetic one who helped her make new memories and feel good about her own life. But I'd spent all my resources before I even got there. In my need to be perfectly Good, I'd gotten my priorities all mixed up and I'd lost sight of how important it is, with any one of your values, to start at home.

It means far less for someone to outwardly preach the values of Good personhood if they don't also embody those values with the people around them. We shouldn't be underestimating the Goodness that comes from supporting our friends, family and community. The

Goodness that is created when we are Good to each other and Good in our own little worlds is what ripples out and carries the greater Good out there. Every bit of Goodness counts.

When I was consumed with being a morally perfect person, I was a worse friend, a worse sister, a worse partner, a worse daughter. In my desperation to be Good (according to an impossible standard), I'd lost sight of the everyday acts of Goodness that used to anchor my life. And it was time to prioritise them again.

I started to spend less of my energy on trying to be morally perfect, and more of it on making memories with my sister. I decided that when I'm with her, being a Good sister is the most important kind of Goodness that I could embody. Nobody gets to tell me otherwise.

I gave myself permission to spend less time endlessly doomscrolling into every Bad thing happening in the world. I could stay informed, do my part, and also set some boundaries to protect my own well-being. Yes, it is a privilege to be able to look away, but we cannot be helpful to anyone or anything if we're consumed by tragedy and hopelessness all day every day. If we want to be Good, first, we need to be okay.

I realised that I can strive to make ethical and sustainable choices, and also not bury myself in guilt when I don't get it right every single time. Sometimes it rains, and you make a choice based on the options you have in sight.

I still care deeply about the world and want it to be a safer, more just place, but I know that holding myself to an impossible standard of moral perfection isn't the way to get there. I know that the real, sustainable work is done in community, and it doesn't require a few perfect people, it requires lots of imperfect ones.

I'm no longer willing to believe that I am Bad, simply because I exist. I'm not a perfectly Good person either. I am a person who tries their best to be Good, whilst recognising their own limitations, and not sacrificing their sanity in the process. And I've decided that's more than Good enough.

LIKEABILITY

"Don't you think it's strange," I said to a friend in the shaded courtyard of a café, "that fictional characters can be so flawed, and do so much wrong, and we'll still root for them. We'll still *like* them on some level – especially if they're men... But in real life, it feels like you have to be completely perfect in order to be likeable – especially if you're a woman?"

I'd just finished watching Penn Badgley's portrayal of the undeniably charismatic main character in the Netflix thriller, *You*. The internet had been overrun with declarations of love for Joe Goldberg. Despite the fact that he's a stalker and a serial killer, we were all still, bizarrely, rooting for his happiness. We *liked* the guy.

On the other side of my online world, an influencer had shared some of the brutal comments she'd found written about her on a gossip forum, attacking everything from her weight to her voice and how fake she must be underneath her friendly persona.

I couldn't help but see it as a perfect example of how much harder women have it when it comes to likeability – it's a game that we consistently lose, despite lifetimes spent trying to figure out how to win.

I have always wanted, more than is humanly healthy, to be liked. If I imagine flicking a switch that would make every person in this world have a positive opinion of me, the relief that washes over my body is palpable. If I'm liked, then I'm safe. If I'm liked, then I'm valuable. If I'm liked, then I'm getting it right.

I've felt this way since the first social interactions I can remember. I always wanted the most friends at school and to be every teacher's favourite. I wanted to be likeable to the boys but not so much that I was unlikeable to the girls. I wanted every first impression to be perfect and every interaction to display the very best of who I was. I wanted to be liked by everyone.

When I was six years old, I felt like I'd cracked the code: if you have long hair, share your colourful gel pens and go along with whatever your new potential friend wants to talk about, it will lead to them liking you enough to want to sit next to you at lunch. If you do the same thing the next day, suddenly, you have more than one friend! Such a simple formula! But like most things, the older you get, the more complicated it becomes.

As women, we have collected endless mixed messages about what it means to be likeable: be beautiful, but not so beautiful that you're threatening to other women. Be polite but not so polite that you're just a pushover. Be successful but don't be so ambitious that you become intimidating. Be funny but don't make yourself the centre of attention. Be humble but not so self-deprecating that it gets annoying. Be intelligent but don't make anyone else feel less intelligent. Wear the right clothes – no, not those; yes, those, but not like that. Help everyone but don't complain about being tired. Don't let yourself go but don't try too hard. Be mothers but don't make it your whole personality. Smile. Always smile. No matter what you're doing: smile.

I feel like I have been studying likeability since I first understood that it mattered. Years and years of data collection on which women were likeable and practising how to embody their same traits. I'm still figuring out which parts of my personality are really me, and which are parts I've cultivated to placate the opinions of everyone around me. Who would we be, if we weren't so terrified of not being liked?

Somewhere between childhood and where I am now, the weight of needing to be liked became unbearably heavy. My body would be filled with anxiety before any social interaction. I'd lie awake at night going over and over the details of each conversation from my day, convincing myself that I'd come across terribly and that surely, nobody *really* liked me. I would endlessly monitor everything about myself to make sure I was being as likeable as possible at all times. Being liked wasn't a want, it was a need. Without it, I didn't know who I was.

Wanting to be liked is one of the most natural instincts we have as social beings. It's necessary for our survival – our ancestors would have learned a long time ago that if they weren't likeable enough to be accepted into the group, they were in trouble. Nobody wants to be out on their own in a Palaeolithic winter when it was the other dude in the group who knew how to make fire.

But like all things, there is a space between what is natural and healthy, and what becomes obsessive. Sure, most humans want to be liked to a degree. But then there are those of us who are so consumed by the need to be liked that it keeps us up at night, replaying every moment we could have done differently, using each interaction as evidence of how unlikeable we are.

And while the need to be liked is definitely not gender specific, likeability is a much harder game for women to win.

Not only have we spent a lifetime absorbing conflicting messages about what makes us likeable, the bar is simply higher for us. Or maybe the bar is the same height, but widespread ingrained misogyny means we're starting ten paces behind. Men can show up with half the effort, half the energy, half the empathy, and still earn the title of Good Guy whilst doing the absolute bare minimum. Meanwhile, women bend themselves in half trying to show up perfectly, help everyone, get everything right and will probably still come away with people saying *there's just something about her I don't like... Can't put my finger on it... Just something...*

Too often the criticism comes from other women who've learned that searching for what makes another woman unlikeable might offer them a momentary feeling of superiority. This is one of the few prizes that internalised misogyny offers us: put her down in some way so that you feel slightly better. It wears off quickly and the same thing will come back around and bite you on the arse, but it's still hard to resist taking part.

Likeability for women so often requires a shrinking of something. In order to be likeable to the greatest number, to appeal to the widest swathe of the general population, you have to sand down all of your edges until you have a smooth, frictionless surface. Anything particularly bold or complicated will divide opinion. You must be the human equivalent of vanilla if you want the most people possible to like you: sweet, simple, unoffensive, easy.

There are certain qualities that set off alarm bells in our likeability: anger, overconfidence, outspokenness. Read: anything that deviates away from the baseline expectation of being quiet and docile with a smile on our face. That goes double, triple, quadruple if you're a woman whose identity sits at any intersection that comes with its own load of societal prejudice. Fat women, disabled women, women of colour, trans women, working-class women will have to work even harder to be vanilla enough for the masses, and most of the time, will find that it's impossible.

So, there we are, trying to tone down our complexity, our emotions, our individuality, to win a game that is rigged against us. Maybe that is why being liked becomes such an all-consuming need: we're led to believe that if we just try hard enough, we can win, but in reality, we're thrashing around in quicksand, and we can feel it. That would make anyone obsessive.

Rather than being able to point to anything tangible to explain why it still feels like we're not likeable enough, we're left only being able to blame ourselves. It's all proof of how not enough we are.

No wonder nobody likes us – we don't like us, either.

* * *

Throughout my late teens and into my early twenties, I walked the likeability tightrope of trying to be just enough but never too much of anything. I kept most of my opinions to myself. I went out of my way to not offend anyone. I deferred to everyone else's preferences. I was polite to a fault. I went to social events I didn't really want to go to and kept up with people I didn't really want to be friends with. I smiled nearly constantly. I tried to control my likeability as much as is humanly possible. And still, it never quite felt like I was likeable enough.

When I entered the world of body positivity and started sharing more of myself online, for the first time I was more invested in telling my truth than I was in being liked. I shared my opinions honestly and unapologetically, with less of a filter than I'd had in years. But as the numbers started to creep upwards, so did the pressure to maintain the approval of my new, unexpected audience. It's hard to not care about likeability when your popularity is literally measured in 'likes'.

Still, at least online I could be prepared. I could double-check everything I said for potentially unlikeable phrasing before I put it out. I could hone my persona to only display the very best of myself. I could shape my public image, at least to an extent. I could manage my likeability. I had it all under control... until I didn't.

It happened overnight, literally. I was on holiday, exploring a small Spanish town with my boyfriend at the time. I'd been posting online for nearly a year and I had around two thousand followers – more than I ever imagined I would have, but a number that I felt in control of; I could manage that many perceptions. I could be likeable to that number of people.

I went to bed after a day of walking around cathedrals and eating gelato, and woke up in the early hours of the morning, experiencing sleep paralysis for the first time. I could see the glow of the tiny red dot on the television in our room, and I had the overwhelming feeling that it was watching me. It was coming for me. It was surrounding me. And I couldn't escape.

I finally fully woke up, sweating and hyper-ventilating with my heart trying to escape out of my chest. I tried to explain what had happened to my boyfriend but I couldn't convey the terror. He convinced me to go back to sleep and I dozed fitfully until it was time to get up.

In the daylight I rolled out of bed, exhausted, and began my newly adopted morning routine of checking social media. As soon as I clicked on the little Polaroid camera icon, I knew something had changed. My notifications were flooded with names I didn't recognise, coming in faster than I could process them. I caught single words of paragraph–long comments: 'amazing', 'self-harm', 'obese', 'life-changing'. I clicked onto my own profile; my eyes frantically trying to take it all in. One hundred thousand followers. Increasing by the minute.

A few weeks earlier, I'd agreed to have a conversation with a local journalist who wanted to pitch my story to a few news outlets. "Recovered Anorexic Now Celebrates Belly Rolls Online!" was the first headline I remember seeing, after figuring that nothing was going to come of the interview. In twenty-four hours, the story had been picked up by media platforms all over the world. And the people were coming in faster than I could count: two hundred thousand, three hundred thousand, half a million and rising.

Suddenly, my carefully maintained online diary was being viewed, and commented on, by masses of strangers. More perceptions than I could possibly manage. I was frozen by the fear of what they all might think of whatever I did next. What if I said something they didn't like? What if I let them down? What if they turned on me? How do you maintain being likeable to that many people?!

The answer, of course, is that you can't. It is impossible to be liked by everyone – especially online. But you can sure as hell try.

I went into overdrive trying to please as many people as I could, spending hours overthinking a single post, projecting every potential criticism and tying myself in knots to avoid them. I replied to every single message and comment, suddenly spending ninety percent of my waking hours glued to my phone. I took on board every suggestion, creating more and more to cover all the topics people wanted me to talk about.

If we just keep doing everything perfectly, my brain told me, *then there won't be any reason for people to not like us.*

The first ones to prove my theory wrong were the misogynists: teenage boys with pictures of American flags on their profiles, body-building men who were outraged that I was encouraging other women to not spend their lives sculpting themselves smaller. They poured in with their insults and threats, setting my nervous system to high alert every time I checked my phone.

One day, my account was targeted by an alt-right group who work together online to overwhelm someone's social media with abuse. I sat for hours, deleting comments filled with the most disgusting things that had ever been said about me, blocking thousands of names one by one. I had never been so hated, so openly, by so many people. Their words swirled in my brain for months, following me around, leaving me feeling fragile and hyper-vigilant about what might come next.

Over time, I got more resilient in dealing with that kind of abuse. It was never easy navigating their hatred, but I reasoned that these were not the type of people whose approval I wanted. In fact, if they hated me so much, it probably meant that I was doing something right. They were the first wave who didn't like me, but they weren't my people – I could be disliked by them, and be okay.

Things got trickier when the ones who I *did* think were my people started to dislike me as well.

The larger my account grew, the more criticism I received from inside my community: a comment here, an unfollow there, an accusatory message about all the things I was doing wrong. A blog post questioning my intentions, a video filled with made-up facts that made me problematic, a co-ordinated cancellation campaign encouraging people to turn against me.

All at once, the thing that I had spent my entire life trying to avoid was happening: people didn't like me. Most of them strangers, some of them friends, each disapproval crashing down on my chest. My body went into a state of pure panic; I was being rejected by the group. It felt like the sun was coming down and I was about to be left outside to fend for myself in the wilderness.

I did everything I could to change their minds – more of whatever they said they wanted. I became more and more self-deprecating, apologising for everything about myself and agreeing that yes, I was the problem and yes, I would do better. It didn't matter. Every day I braced myself for more reasons why I was unlikeable, and every day I gave a bit more of my self-esteem away, trying to change people's minds.

Around that time, I agreed to have lunch with someone from my online world who I'd always looked up to. They were one of the original body acceptance bloggers, an inspiration to me and countless others. As soon as I read their invite I was filled with dread, questioning how they could possibly want to be my friend when I was clearly so awful.

Agreeing to meet them was risky. Maybe they only wanted to meet me so they could tell me in person how worthless I was... Or maybe they wouldn't turn up at all? Maybe they'd turn up with *other* people who also didn't like me and collectively tear me to shreds right there, over a plate of avocado toast. By the time the day arrived, I must have had enough adrenaline running through my body to last me a lifetime.

They were lovely. Warm, curious and an excellent hugger. They sensed my social anxiety and reassured me that they were so happy to finally be meeting in real life. We talked for hours, eventually getting onto the topic of social media, and how we both handle the pressures that come with it. I listened, flabbergasted, as they told me how many people – strangers and friends – had turned against them online over the years. I couldn't understand how anyone could dislike this person. They were a fucking delight.

I decided that it was safe to be vulnerable, and admit how much of a toll not being liked on such a huge scale had taken on my mental health. And that despite it all: the days spent scrolling through hate, the panic attacks, the hours in therapy, the shattered self-esteem, I still couldn't seem to let it go. I still needed to be liked. I asked them what the secret was – how were they here, speaking so freely about something that felt like the end of the world to me?

They took a long drink of their lemonade, and looked at me as if they were deciphering whether I could handle what they were about to say next:

"Megan, people won't like you, and you will live."

I froze, fork in mid-air, trying to swallow the enormity of the statement. The first part sent a grip of panic through my body: *people won't like you.* They'd said it so casually, like it was an inevitability that I'd just have to accept. But I wasn't ready to accept it yet.

My brain jumped into action to figure out new ways to prevent it from being true. *No, I can absolutely get everyone to like me! If I just turn myself into exactly what they want... If I just avoid ever sharing my opinion... If I just change the way I speak, and look, and think... I can make everyone like me!* But I knew, even as I was thinking it, that I'd tried it all already, and here I was.

I was hoping that this person – who had been through the same things that I had – would be able to give me the secret to changing people's minds. I was hoping for another part of the story where they revealed that now, all the people who didn't like them before saw who they really were and adored them! They were all the best of friends!

Instead, I got the confronting, undeniable truth: some people won't like me, and I will live. I will survive it. I will continue to be. I will get up and I will make things. I will go to cafes with people and have conversations. I will hug dogs and smile when I see something beautiful. People won't like me, and it won't destroy me. Or at least, *it will only destroy me if I let it.*

The reality of not being liked by someone is miles away from what our brain imagines and what our body braces itself for. When we know someone doesn't like us, it can be such an all-consuming feeling that we assume their hatred of us is also all-consuming. In reality, they might spend a tiny portion of their day saying negative things about us or thinking negative thoughts. It is very rarely as big of a deal as our anxious brains make it out to be. We can choose to fixate on the person and their dislike of us, or we can go about our lives, focusing on the things that *we* like, and giving our energy to the people who like us.

And I know, that's easier said than done. Because when somebody doesn't like us, it hurts. Of course, it does. It hurts to be unfairly judged. It hurts to be misunderstood. It hurts to be rejected. But the largest hurt comes from within, when we choose to believe what those people think of us, rather than standing in our own knowledge of who we are.

There is *nobody* in this world who knows you better than you do. There is nobody else who has been with you through every moment, navigated every challenge, felt every emotion, heard every thought. You are the only person who you will be with for your entire life. You are the only person who knows exactly who you are.

How could people who barely know you, who see a tiny fraction of something that represents you, who have misunderstood your character because of their own biases and projections, have the authority to tell you who you are and how you should feel about yourself? The idea that they know you better than you is absurd.

And the thing about people's opinions of you is that they are not formed on a blank slate. Whenever someone meets you, they are carrying with them everything that's ever happened to them. Every preconception they might already have. Every emotion they're experiencing in that moment. Every trauma, defence mechanism, every belief they have about themselves. Very few people enter an interaction with a mind completely open to seeing who the other person might be. Sometimes, our opinion of other people is whatever we need it to be, to protect us in some way.

About a year ago, I got a rogue message on Instagram from someone whose username I vaguely recognised. The first line read "I need to apologise to you."

The person went on to reveal how they had hate-followed me for years, leaving horrible comments under my posts and even joining forums with other people who all discussed how much they didn't like me.

"I've said so many awful things about you and it was fucked up," the message read, "I realise now that when

I found you, when I saw you being happy and carefree in your body, it was too confronting for me. I was so deep in the self-hatred. And I was jealous that you weren't. I hated you because I wasn't ready to see you and I'm sorry."

I had to read the message a few times to fully process what they'd said. In the past, finding out that someone had openly disliked me for so long would have broken me, but knowing that their dislike of me came from their own insecurity took the power right out of it. And I didn't feel angry or resentful towards the person, because I understood. I've made enemies out of others for similar reasons. I've disliked people because I've been jealous of something they have, or because they've reflected a part of myself that's uncomfortable for me to see.

Sometimes people won't like us because we are a mirror to something in themselves that they're not ready to look at. Sometimes people will project whatever they're going through onto us, turn us into a scapegoat for their difficult emotions. Some people won't trust that we are who we say we are, because they've been burned too many times already.

Should we take those people's opinions of us as fact? Should we buy into their narrative, knowing that it's tainted, incomplete or inaccurate? Why on Earth would we give their opinion more weight than our own? Why would we hand our self-esteem over to them?

You might be thinking that if someone doesn't like you, based on things that aren't really true, then the solution is to simply change their mind! Open wide, this one's hard to swallow: if someone doesn't like you, it is not your job to change their mind. It is not your duty to gain their approval. It is not your responsibility to make sure that they have an accurate picture of you.

Your job is to know yourself well enough, that when someone doesn't see you clearly, it doesn't shake how you see yourself. Your job is to be so sure of who you are, that nobody can take that knowing away from you. Your job is to like yourself. And to carry on living as your whole self, regardless of the opinions that might come to throw you off your path.

It's probably worth noting that sometimes people won't like us for valid reasons. Sometimes someone's negative opinion of us might be a prompt for us to take an honest look at ourselves and see where we could do better. But I'm writing this from the assumption that the majority of us are not arseholes, but are generally good people who do their best and care too much about what others think of them.

We like to think that we can control how other people see us. Especially in this time and place of cultivating our outward presence and sharing our lives more publicly than we ever have. We believe that we can, and should, craft the most perfectly likeable representations of our-selves in order to gain public approval. There is safety in believing that we can secure positive opinion, if we just do exactly the right things. There is comfort in the idea of that control.

But other people's thoughts have always been out of our control. What they like, what they believe, their opinions have never been ours to dictate. In a very simple way, other people's thoughts are not our business. Which means that what other people think of us, is not our business.

Whether we are liked by everyone doesn't have to be what we hinge our value on. It can't be, if we want a chance at feeling okay about ourselves. Because what other people think of us, ultimately, has very little to do with us, and everything to do with them.

* * *

Right now, I can tell you with certainty that there are people who do not like me.

There are people who spend their time actively disliking me: going out of their way to leave cruel comments or spread harmful gossip online. There are people who haven't liked me since childhood, holding onto a narrative we've both long outgrown. There are people who do not like me simply because of what I represent: a chubby, mixed-race, queer woman with feminist values. All of these people are a blessing.

All of them have provided me with the opportunity to lean further into knowing myself, accepting myself, and being on my own side.

Every person with an inaccurate view of who I am has helped me know myself better.

Every person who has hated me based on their own insecurity has taught me to let go.

Every person who has seen me and decided that I am not for them has cleared the way for the people who will see me and decide that I am. Those people won't find me unless I'm being myself – even if that version of me is unlikeable to others.

I no longer lie awake at night replaying my conversations and worrying about whether I was likeable enough in all of my interactions. I know that as long as I showed up as my whole self, that was enough. Whatever opinions people formed of me based on me being myself are none of my business.

I am no longer scared of not being liked. I am far more scared of spending my life showing up as someone I'm not just so that people will like me. I won't sacrifice myself for the fleeting approval of anyone else. I won't base my worth on how likeable I am to everyone but me.

And because I have gotten to this place: been confronted with not being liked, been destroyed by it, learned from it, and rebuilt myself again, I can finally say that I like myself. And that feels better than being liked by the whole world.

SELF-LOVE

Is there anything to say on the topic of self-love that hasn't been said before?

There isn't a woman left in this world who hasn't been told a cliché quote on the importance of loving herself, or been sold a cliché solution to loving herself more. We don't need any more bath bombs, candles or overpriced beauty procedures in order to practise self-love. Those things are nice, but ultimately, there's more to self-love than what can be bought.

The greatest acts of self-love are often the least aesthetic, and the least commodifiable. They are sometimes boring, often hard. My greatest acts of self-love are ones I've shared with you in these pages: unlearning cultural messages that kept me small, ending relationships where my heart wasn't safe, understanding my own wounds and tending to them again and again until they've started to heal.

They haven't always been pretty or even easy for other people to understand. And that's okay, other people don't have to understand the ways we heal.

The ultimate challenge in my own practice of self-love has always been allowing myself to believe that I deserve it. I have been an expert at finding reasons why I am an exception to the rule when it comes to self-love. *Of course,* everybody else deserves to be kind to themselves and respect their needs! But not me. *Obviously, nobody should feel like a failure or an awful person just because they're not perfect!* Except me, I'm awful. Everyone is entitled to feel good things! Everyone bar one.

My brain has provided me with endless reasons why I don't deserve to treat myself lovingly:

I haven't done enough. I'm not productive enough or successful enough. I don't work hard enough.

The world is on fire! How selfish would I have to be to focus on my own well-being when there is so much pain and horror happening?

If I start being nice to myself then I'll never reach my goals or get any better as a person!

I believed, for a long while, that I could hate myself into a version of myself I would love. I told myself that denying myself joy was the least I could do to recognise my privilege and show that I cared about the world. I thought that self-hate was the greatest motivator. I was so wrong.

Self-love is the only option if we want to survive with ourselves. There is no other choice but to offer ourselves kindness, even when we get something wrong. We have to care for ourselves, even when we feel like we don't deserve it. We need to be on our own side, because life will be challenging enough without being our own worst enemy.

And in case you're reading this and thinking that it's true for everyone else, but not for you: you are not the exception.

For years, I've chipped away at all the reasons my brain provides as proof that we are not allowed to love ourselves. And some of them are incredibly convincing! But underneath them all, way down deep, is a belief that not only am I undeserving of that love, but in fact I am deserving of self-punishment.

Whether it's been impossible beauty standards, unrealistic expectations of productivity, or the pressure of moral perfectionism, the root is always the same. These are things that I have used as proof that I am not enough, in one way or another, and I should therefore be punished.

Punished with crash diets and over-exercising, punished by working myself to the point of burn out, punished by withholding my own right to happiness and not allowing myself to be okay. Why? What could I have possibly done to be deserving of such consistent self-harm?

The answer, of course, is nothing. Nothing except exist. And be human – limited, imperfect.

Nobody in this world should believe that they are worthy of punishment simply because they exist.

And the only way to create a new narrative is to practise.

Every time that you reclaim a part of yourself that you were taught to see as a flaw, you are practising self-love. Every time you set a boundary that preserves your well-being, you are practising self-love. Every time you refuse to keep carrying the shame that was never meant to be yours, you are practising self-love. Every time you listen to your inner child, listen to your body, listen to your heart, listen to your wisdom, and put their suggestions in place, you are practising self-love.

And it is a practice. There is no one-time quick fix shortcut to loving yourself. Especially when we're battling against a lifetime of believing we aren't enough. But we are strong enough, and smart enough, and bold enough to do things differently. Anyone who has endured the endless onslaught of cultural messaging on all the ways we are not enough and has managed to survive, has the resilience and the tenacity to build a more loving internal world for themselves. That is the very least we deserve.

Treating myself lovingly is still unfamiliar. In a way, I am much more comfortable with self-punishment – I know it better. It doesn't feel good but it feels normal, and safe. I know what to expect down here, where I'm convinced that I'm worthless and undeserving of anything good. It is harder to resist those well-worn pathways and be nice to myself than it is to keep being harsh.

But I have done harder things than this. I have unlearned more destructive habits than this. I have grown into new versions of myself again and again, and I can grow into this, too. I can practise loving myself until it doesn't feel like practice anymore, until it's the only way I know how to be.

Writing this book has been a practice of self-love. I have had to defy my inner critic who tells me that I have nothing valuable to say. I have had to resist my past perfectionist ways that wouldn't allow me to put anything into the world unless I believed it was the best of the best of the best. I've had to be soft with myself when the things I've written about have taken me back to painful places, and allow myself to rest, restore and come back again.

I hope that something you've read in these pages has inspired you to be more loving towards yourself. To forgive yourself. To advocate for yourself. To understand yourself.

I hope that when we look back on our lives, the choices we made, how we treated ourselves, the ways we healed, we will be able to say that everything came from a place of loving ourselves. I hope we will be able to say that we didn't make ourselves smaller, here.

ACKNOWLEDGEMENTS

I am endlessly grateful to every person who has helped to bring this book to life. To the team at Catalyst for their incredible hard work, my brilliant literary agent Rachel Mills, to Kim and the Diving Bell team, and to all my friends, family and my wonderful partner for supporting me along the way.

My deepest gratitude goes to you, the reader. Thank you for picking up this book, for allowing me to share my thoughts and feelings with you. Some of you have been supporting my work for years now, and I cannot tell you how much that means to me. Thank you for being here, for being who you are, and for believing in a world where we don't have to keep making ourselves small.

ENDNOTES

1. León, María Pilar et al. "What Do Children Think of Their Perceived and Ideal Bodies? Understandings of Body Image at Early Ages: A Mixed Study." *International Journal of Environmental Research and Public Health*, vol. 18, no. 9: 4871, 2021, doi:10.3390/ijerph18094871.
2. Miller, Kelsey. "Study: Most Girls Start Dieting By Age 8." Refinery29, 2015, https://www.refinery29.com/en-us/2015/01/81288/children-dieting-body-image.
3. Aung, Toe and Leah Williams. "Mirror, mirror on the wall: Whose figure is the fairest of them all?" *Evolutionary Behavioral Sciences*, vol. 13, no. 4, 2019, pp. 387–393. Accessed via APA PsychNet, https://psycnet.apa.org/record/2018-59970-001.
4. Watson, Stephanie et al. "What Is the Waist-to-Hip Ratio?" Edited by John Bassham and Angela M. Bell, MD. *Healthline*, 2021, https://www.healthline.com/health/waist-to-hip-ratio.
5. Maine, Margo. ""Get Real Barbie" Fact Sheet." *Body Wars: Making Peace With Women's Bodies*, Gurze Books, 2000.
6. Harriger, Jennifer A. et al. "You can buy a child a curvy Barbie doll, but you can't make her like it: Young girls' beliefs about Barbie dolls with diverse shapes and sizes." *Body Image*, vol. 30, 2019, pp. 107–113, doi:10.1016/j.bodyim.2019.06.005.
7. Jones, Chelsea C. and Stacy L. Young. "The Mother-Daughter Body Image Connection: The Perceived Role of Mothers' Thoughts, Words, and Actions." *Journal of Family Communication*, vol. 21, no. 2, 2021, pp. 118–126. Accessed via Taylor & Francis Online, https://www.tandfonline.com/doi/abs/10.1080/15267431.2021.1908294. Benyo, Lauren. "Influence of Mothers on the Development of Body Dissatisfaction Influence of Mothers on the Development of Body Dissatisfaction in Daughters." *Intuition: The BYU Undergraduate Journal of Psychology Intuition: The BYU Undergraduate Journal of Psychology*, vol. 12, no. 1, 2017, pp. 175–196, https://scholarsarchive.

byu.edu/cgi/viewcontent.cgi?article=1025&context=intuition. Handford, Charlotte M., et al. "The influence of maternal modeling on body image concerns and eating disturbances in preadolescent girls." *Behaviour Research and Therapy*, vol. 100, 2018, pp. 17–23, https://www.sciencedirect.com/science/article/abs/pii/S0005796717302309.

8. AnyBody UK. "Making An Informed Decision: Your Guide To The National Child Measurement Programme", AnyBody UK, 2022, https://anybodyuk.org/wp-content/uploads/2024/11/Play-Not-Weigh-2.pdf. Humphreys, Stephen. "The unethical use of BMI in contemporary general practice." *The British Journal of General Practice: The Journal of the Royal College of General Practitioners,* vol. 60,578, 2010, pp. 696–7, doi:10.3399/bjgp10X515548. Pray, Rachel, and Suzanne Riskin. "The History and Faults of the Body Mass Index and Where to Look Next: A Literature Review." *Cureus,* vol. 15, no. 11, e48230, 2023, doi:10.7759/cureus.48230.

9. Altman, Emily et al. "Weight Measurements in School: Setting and Student Comfort." *Journal of Nutrition Education and Behavior,* vol. 54, no.3, 2022, pp. 249 – 254, doi:10.1016/j.jneb.2021.11.007. Bacon, Linda, and Lucy Aphramor. "Weight science: evaluating the evidence for a paradigm shift." *Nutrition Journal,* vol. 10, no. 9, 2011, doi:10.1186/1475-2891-10-9.

10. Rathbone, Joanne A. et al. "Rethinking the public health approach to obesity." The British Psychological Society, 2020, https://www.bps.org.uk/psychologist/rethinking-public-health-approach-obesity.

11. Komar, Marlen. "Photos Of Shaving Ads From The Last 100 Years." *Bustle,* 26 January 2016, https://www.bustle.com/articles/137072-100-years-of-shaving-ads-show-how-weve-been-tricked-into-going-hairless-photos.

12. Boserio, Gail. "Getting plucked: the history of hair removal." *ABC,* 10 March 2015, https://www.abc.net.au/listen/programs/latenightlive/get-plucked:-the-history-of-hair-removal/6293450.

13. Iglikowski-Broad, Vicky. *Section 28: impact, fightback and repeal,* 2023. Accessed via The National Archives, https://beta.nationalarchives.gov.uk/explore-the-collection/stories/section-28-impact-fightback-repeal/.

14. Stonewall UK. "Key dates for lesbian, gay, bi and trans equality." Stonewall UK, 2021, https://www.stonewall.org.uk/resources/key-dates-lesbian-gay-bi-and-trans-equality.

15. Reality Check Team, BBC UK. "Homosexuality: The countries where it is illegal to be gay." *BBC News*, 31 March 2023, https://www.bbc.co.uk/news/world-43822234. Bandera, Gerardo. "Which countries impose the death penalty on gay people?" Fair Planet, 13 July 2024, https://www.fairplanet.org/story/death-penalty-homosexualty-illegal/.

16. Goodier, Michael. "Hate crimes against transgender people hit record high in England and Wales." *Guardian*, 5 October 2023, https://www.theguardian.com/society/2023/oct/05/record-rise-hate-crimes-transgender-people-reported-england-and-wales.

17. Flo Health. "Mind the gaps: Menstrual and reproductive misinformation in the UK in 2023." Flo Health, 2023, https://flo.health/landings/reproductive-health-report-uk.

18. Beccia, Carlyn. "The Grim History of Slut-Shaming." Medium, The Grim Historian, 7 March 2023, https://medium.com/grimhistorian/the-grim-history-of-slut-shaming-d053c5986801.

19. Lister, Kate. "A brief history of how brutal interrogations of 'witches' were all about punishing sex." *i Paper*, 30 October 2018, https://inews.co.uk/opinion/columnists/a-brief-history-of-how-interrogations-of-witches-were-all-about-sex-215626.

20. Lister, Kate. "Female masturbation and the perils of pleasure." *Wellcome Collection*, 27 February 2019, https://wellcomecollection.org/stories/female-masturbation-and-the-perils-of-pleasure.

21. United Nations. "International Day of Zero Tolerance for Female Genital Mutilation, 6 February." United Nations, 2025, https://www.un.org/en/observances/female-genital-mutilation-day.

22. Smith, Matthew, and Eir Nolsoe. "The orgasm gap: 61% of men, but only 30% of women, say they orgasm every time they have sex." YouGov UK, 2022, https://yougov.co.uk/society/articles/40941-orgasm-gap-61-men-only-30-women-say-they-orgasm-ev

23. Relate UK. "'Milestone anxiety' on the rise among millennials and Gen Z." Relate UK, 2022, https://www.relate.org.uk/get-help/milestone-anxiety-rise-among-millennials-and-gen-z.

24. Kemp, Simon. "The time we spend on social media." DataReportal, 31 January 2024, https://datareportal.com/reports/digital-2024-deep-dive-the-time-we-spend-on-social-media

25. Ibbetson, Connor. "Why do people choose to not have children?" YouGov UK, 9 January 2020, https://yougov.co.uk/society/articles/25364-why-are-britons-choosing-not-have-children

26. Campbell, Denis. "Record numbers of women reach 30 child-free in England and Wales." *Guardian*, 27 January 2022, https://

www.theguardian.com/lifeandstyle/2022/jan/27/women-child-free-30-ons.

27. Brown, Jessica. "How much does it cost to raise a child in the UK?" *The Times*, 16 February 2024, https://www.thetimes.com/money-mentor/income-budgeting/family-finance/starting-family-baby-costs.

28. Jones, Rozi. "Income to house price ratio more than doubles since the 70s." *Financial Reporter*, 5 July 2023, https://www.financialreporter.co.uk/income-to-house-price-ratio-more-than-doubles-since-the-70s.html. Bolt Insight. "18–30's UK Finance". Bolt Insights, 2023, https://www.boltinsight.com/wp-content/uploads/2023/10/Bolt-Factor-18-30s-UK-Finance.pdf.

29. Malinsky, Gili. "57% of Gen Zers want to be influencers—but 'it's constant, Monday through Sunday,' says creator." *CNBC*, 14 September 2024, https://www.cnbc.com/2024/09/14/more-than-half-of-gen-z-want-to-be-influencers-but-its-constant.html.

30. Clemo, Freddie. "Two thirds of workers fear burnout and believe businesses prioritise profit over people, report finds." People Management, 17 January 2025, https://www.peoplemanagement.co.uk/article/1902740/two-thirds-workers-fear-burnout-believe-businesses-prioritise-profit-people-report-finds.

20948682R00086

Printed in Great Britain
by Amazon